D1382747

DONNE

THE CRAFTSMAN

An Essay upon the Structure of the

SONGS and SONNETS

DONNE

THE CRAFTSMAN

An Essay upon the Structure of the

SONGS and SONNETS

by PIERRE LEGOUIS

Docteur es-Lettres

NEW YORK

RUSSELL & RUSSELL · INC

1962

FIRST PUBLISHED IN FRANCE IN 1928
L. C. CATALOG CARD NO: 62—10232

PRINTED IN THE UNITED STATES OF AMERICA

PREFACE

_____

*In medieval epics the son often begot his father : of
Guillaume au Court Nez, for instance, came Aimeri de
Narbonne. A somewhat similar relationship* (si parva ma-
gnis componere licet) *obtains between the present essay
on Donne and my book on Marvell. The study of the disciple led me to the study of the master. In a chapter of
my larger work I introduced the first of the « metaphysical » poets to French readers who, by hypothesis, knew
little or nothing about him. I therefore insisted on his
most conspicuous and important characteristics, his intensity of feeling, originality and subtlety of thought. So far
I found myself in agreement with the criticism of to-day.
But here, at the cost of an apparent contradiction, I submit to readers already familiar with Donne's poetry
and conversant with the literature of the subject that the
prevalent view is incomplete and unconsciously biassed,
that there still remain unexplored regions in this varied
personality. Looking at my demonstration a last time before I commit it to print, I feel more confident than ever
that my main contention is right, but also realize that a
much better exponent than myself would have been required to give it its full chance. The former part of this
essay will prove, I fear, dull to most readers on account of*

its minute technicalities, while the little band of seriously-minded persons who persevere may think the latter part frivolous, if not indecorous. The dullness is all my own, but for the levity Donne alone is responsible; at any rate I have brought none to this examination of his poetry.

A bibliography will not be expected at the end of so short and restricted a study as this. I have tried to acknowledge particular obligations wherever I have incurred them, with one exception : the history of English literature lately written by Professors Emile Legouis and Louis Cazamian does not appear either in text or notes ; but one cannot fail to see that this essay develops some hints thrown out in the pages there devoted to Donne. As regards Professor Grierson, though I shall often mention him in the following pages, I must not pass over in this place my general indebtedness to him : not only has the text of his edition, which may well be called final, formed the basis of my acquaintance with Donne (I have reproduced it in all my quotations), not only have his notes opened to me the meaning of many perplexed passages ; but without his successive probings of the poet's heart and brain, ever more deep-reaching, I could never have undertaken this work. The minor differences between my views and his, hereafter insisted upon almost unduly, weigh little against my admiring agreement with the bulk of his criticism. I have also to thank Professor René Huchon, of the Sorbonne, for advice and encouragement, both when I chose this subject and after he had read the manuscript. Mr. H. M. Margoliouth, M. A. Oxon., formerly Professor in the University College of Southampton, and Mr. David Spens Steuart, B. A. London, lecteur in the

*University of Besançon, kindly helped me with sug-
gestions which made the expression of my ideas less
imperfect.* The Maison de l'Institut de France *in London
offered me in* 1925 *an hospitality which facilitated the
preparation for the writing of this essay.*

PIERRE LEGOUIS.

Besançon, March 1928.

ERRATA

P. 12, ll. 3-4,	instead of	hang-ging	read	hang-ing
P. 21, l. 22,	—	Il is only	—	It is only
P. 22, l. 6,	—	The Sum	—	The Sun
P. 23, l. 3	—	Love> — the	—	Love>) — the
P. 23, l. 5,	—	Extasie — the	—	Extasie) — the
P. 26, l. 32,	—	Il any	—	If any
P. 28., l. 10,	—	wake him thinke	—	wake him, thinke
P. 36, l. 23,	—	words	—	works
P. 37, n. 24, l. 2,	—	Soe	—	See
P. 43, l. 17,	—	di grow	—	did grow
P. 44, l. 14,	—	that he	—	that the
— —	—	for	—	or
P. 46, l. 8,	—	contradictoy	—	contradictory
P. 52, l. 26,	—	On, that's	—	Oh, that's
P. 59, l. 6	—	more than	—	more than
P. 61, l. 19	—	none of then	—	none of them
— l. 29	—	occuring	—	occurring
P. 63, ll. 17-18	—	preser-ves	—	pre-serves
P. 63, n. 36, l. 7	—	vers ; he	—	vers, he
P. 75, n. 42, l. 6	—	not title	—	no title
P. 77, l. 15	—	woman's	—	the woman's
P. 28, l. 24,	instead of	hate vould	read	hate would
P. 63, l. 10,	—	out, hung	—	out,) hung
P. 67, l. 4,	—	Through	—	Though
P. 70, n. 39, l. 22,	—	summun	—	summum
P. 79, l. 20,	—	full-lengh	—	full-length

CORRIGENDA

P. 18, 1 10 G. Gregory Smith in his *Elizabethan critical essays* prints « favour » instead of « savour » in this passage.

P. 23, l. 7. Saintsbury however says (*History of English prosody*, I. 352) that this stanza « is one often used by Spenser's predecessors (especially his immediate predecessors) ». — Paul Verrier, *Essai sur les principes de la métrique anglaise* (Paris, 1909), Ire partie, p. 253, says that this stanza is one of the forms of the Tuscan *rispetto* and was imported into England « à la Renaissance ».

DONNE THE CRAFTSMAN

An essay upon the structure of the
Songs and Sonets

For the last hundred years the fame of Donne has
been growing steadily. Indeed recent criticism is making
him ample amends for long neglect or detraction. Even
the more abstruse and forbidding of his prose works are
reprinted, and his poetry has lost much of its proverbial
« obscureness » since fortune, at last kind, provided it
with such editors as Professor Norton, Sir Edmund Chambers, and, above all, Professor Grierson. His life has been
written by Sir Edmund Gosse with the critic's own charm
and knowledge of human nature. Miss Ramsay has helped us to an easier understanding of that which is most
alien to the modern mind in Donne's culture, his scholastic training. Quite lately an Italian writer, Signor Mario
Praz, has introduced him to his fellow-countrymen in a
book which well deserves to be read by Englishmen (1).
It looks to-day as if it were both presumptuous and super-
fluous to tackle again the central problem of the poet's
relation to his poetry, especially in his best and best-

---

(1) *Secentismo e Marinismo in Inghilterra, John Donne — Richard
Crashaw*. Firenze. « La Voce », 1925.

known work, the *Songs and Sonets*. Yet, while no bran-
new interpretation is offered here, I propose to insist
on one aspect of Donne's talent which seems to have been
overlooked or at least insufficiently recognized. More
than justice has been done to his earnestness on the one
hand, to his extensive and thorough acquaintance with
medieval philosophy on the other hand, but the trans-
mutation of both personal experience and recondite learning
into lyrical poetry has not been paid its due share of attention. Art has not unfrequently been denied in order to
enhance the value of its time-honoured antithesis, nature.
Even Signor Praz, whose criticism usually is as balanced
as it is brilliant, seems to have overshot the mark in his
implicit comparison of Donne to Mount Vesuvius and of
his poetry to the lava pouring out therefrom, while the
minor *metaphysical* poets are likened to « the Neapolitan
craftsman who collects it hard and cold and carves it into
pipe-bowls and objects of vertu » (2). Witty as it is, the
comparison exaggerates the difference between master and
pupils. But perhaps the most characteristic and unqualified expression of this tendency to see in Donne only the
inspired, almost the possessed, thinker, is to be found
in a recent interesting book entitled *Poetic imagery illus-
trated from Elizabethan literature*, by Mr. Henry W.
Wells (3). The American scholar, while ranking Donne
very high, speaks of his intensity of feeling as being so
insistent that it becomes « perhaps even inartistic », and
adds : « From his ardent intensity, not from an itching to
be a wit or from over-consciousness as an artist, came

---

(2) *The Modern language review*, July 1926, p. 320.
(3) Columbia University Press, New-York, 1924.

his rugged lines and Radical metaphors » (4). (By the epithet « Radical », Mr. Wells means very much what Johnson condemned as « metaphysical »). In its anxiety to clear Donne of the charge of artificiality, this appreciation runs to the other extreme and makes him a sort of romantic genius, uncouth and unkempt, who cared nothing for the form of poetry so long as he could unlock his heart with the key, not of the regular sonnet, but of the irregular lyric.

Is it possible, without going back to classical standards, to test the poetry of Donne, neither as an outburst of feeling nor as a produce of the intellect that deals in abstractions (both of which it undoubtedly is), but for the nonce merely as the work of a gifted, restless, unequal, yet highly conscious craftsman ? This last word fits my purpose well because of its modesty, while « artist » might require a preliminary sifting of the many and widely divergent definitions of art left us by the XIXth century. I need not commit myself to any one theory in particular, but I especially disavow the limitation of the artistic to the beautiful. Aim, purpose, intention, is what I am primarily concerned with, though I may pass judgements, secondarily, on the quality of the art, or craftsmanship, or technique, three words between which I shall not distinguish. Another preliminary warning is requisite : style in its narrower sense, *i. e.* diction, I shall leave out of reckoning, except as it is related to the arrangement and effect of each piece taken as a whole. There is enough, as I trust, in the structure of the *Songs and Sonets* to bear out my contention.

---

(4) P. 128.

*
* *

First comes up for examination Donne's metrical practice. Ever since Ben Jonson passed his famous sentence « that Donne for not keeping of accent deserved hanging », it has been a commonplace of criticism that the iambic rhythm suffers much at the hands of the rebel poet. Indeed some critics have proffered the theory that the « not keeping of accent », whether felicitous or not in its results, was deliberate. I shall go one step further and add that it was rather reactionary than revolutionary ; Donne tried to revert to a freedom that English poetry had lost for less than twenty years. An appendix will provide such as are interested in the problem with some evidence pointing that way. But it is unnecessary to examine it here for two reasons. First, as Mr. Saintsbury has clearly shown, instances of conflict between word-stress and line-rhythm are both numerous and aggressive in the *Satires ;* they are still noticeable in the other heroic couplets of Donne ; but in the *Songs and Sonets*, with which only we are concerned, they hardly ever occur (5). Secondly, prosody in its stricter meaning stands in the same relation to metrical structure as diction to composition. Now, just as the conceits have engrossed all the attention which should have been fairly distributed between the various aspects of the writer's art, even so has the wrenching of the stress absorbed the critics of the versifier to such a point that they have neglected almost entirely the other metrical features, especially the build of the stanzas. Therefore prosody, like diction,

---

(5) *A History of English prosody...*, (2nd edition) II, 159.

will be considered only so far as the disposition of syllables in feet affects that of feet in lines, and chiefly that of lines in stanzas, which are the real units (6).

Apart from a chance remark here and there, all the information concerning Donne's use of stanzas is to be extracted out of Professor Schipper's useful books. It will be no reproach to the metrist to say that the student who reads either the larger German work or its English epitome from beginning to end may fail to realise the originality of Donne in this respect. That the members of the poet should be scattered all through the various chapters on *Strophenbau* was a necessity inherent in the general plan. But for that very reason it may not be unprofitable to set before the reader a table of the *Songs and Sonets*, ranged according to the length of the individual stanza in each of them, beginning with the shortest and ending with the most bulky. The distinction between bipartite, tripartite and other stanzas, however important historically, will be disregarded here, since Donne, if he knew the old Provençal rules concerning *frons*, *pedes*, and *cauda*, never troubled to observe them in the forms he invented (7).

---

(6) A fact recognized *en passant* by Mario Praz *Secentismo...*, p. 138 : « l'unità nella poesia del Donne non è il verso, ma la strofa. »

(7) In the following table the figures stand for the number of *syllables* in each line. When Donne substitutes an heptasyllabic for an octosyllabic in one or more stanzas, he avails himself of a time-honoured freedom, and I do not note it here (for other deviations from the pattern, see *infra*). But when he binds himself down to the use of the heptasyllabic all through a piece in the same place in every stanza, he adds to his difficulties, and the table shows it.

That was one reason for not giving the number of *feet*, as in Schipper's system ; another reason was that some at least of Donne's lines will not fall into feet (see *infra*, Appendix A).

COUPLETS :

The Paradox	a^{10} a^6
The Computation	a^{10} a^{10}

QUATRAINS :

The undertaking
[Selfe Love] $\Bigg\}$ a_8 b^6 a^8 b^6

A Feaver
A Valediction : forbidding mourning $\Bigg\}$ a b a b^8
The Extasie

The Baite	a a b b^8
A Jeat Ring sent	a^8 a ^{10} b^{14} b^{10}

SIXAINS :

Communitie	a a b c c b^8
A Valediction : of my name, in the window	a^6 b^{10} a b^8 c^{10} c^8
Breake of day	a a b b^8 c c^{10}
Loves diet	a b^{10} a b^8 c c^{10}
The Expiration	a b a b c c^{10}

SEVEN-LINE STANZAS :

Confined Love	a^8 b^{10} a^8 b^{10} c c^6 c^7
Witchcraft by a picture	a^8 b a^{10} b^8 c^6 c^8 c^{10}
Loves exchange	a^8 a^{10} b^8 b^{10} c c^8 c^{10}
Loves Deitie	a b a b c c^{10} c^8
The good-morrow	a b a b c c^{10} c^{12}

EIGHT-LINE STANZAS :

« *Sweetest love, I do not goe* »	a^7 b^6 a^7 b^6 c^4 d d c^6
The Message	a a b^8 c c d d^3 b^8
Loves Usury	a^{10} a^4 b b c c c^{10} c^4
The Blossome	a^6 b^8 a b c^{10} c^4 d d^{10}

The broken heart	a b a^8 b^{10} c c^8 d d^{10}
The Funerall	a^{10} b^4 a b^{10} c^6 d^{10} c^6 d^{14}
The Legacie	a b b^8 a^{10} a^8 b c c^{10}
The Curse	a b^{10} b^6 a^8 a c c c^{10}
The Dampe	a^{10} a^8 b b^{10} c c^8 d d^{10}
The Prohibition	a^6 a b c b c a a^{10}

NINE-LINE STANZAS :

« *Goe, and catche a falling starre,* »	a b a b c c^7 d d^2 d^7
Negative love	a a b b a b c c c^8
A Valediction : of weeping	a^4 b b a^{10} c c^4 d d^{10} d^{14}
The Canonization	a^{10} b^8 b a^{10} c c^8 c^{10} a^8 a^6
Twicknam garden	a^{10} b a^8 b^{10} b^8 c^{10} c^8 d^{10} d^8
A Valediction : of the booke	a^{10} b^8 b a^{10} c^6 c^7 c^8 d^{10} d^{12}
The Flea	a^8 a^{10} b^8 b^{10} c^8 c^{10} d^8 d d^{10}
A nocturnall	a b^{10} b a^8 c^6 c c d d^{10}
The Indifferent	a^7 b b^{12} a^{10} c c^8 c d d^{10}
The Will	a a b b c^{10} c d^8 d^{10} d^{14}

TEN-LINE STANZAS :

Farewell to love	a^4 a^{10} b^8 c c^{10} b^8 d^2 d e e^{10}
The Sunne Rising	a^8 b^4 b a^{10} c d^8 c d e e^{10}
The Dreame	a b^8 b^4 a^{10} c^8 c d d e e^{10}
The Primrose	a a^6 b b c^{10} c c^8 d d d^{10}
The Anniversarie	a a^8 b b c c^{10} d^8 d d^{10} d^{12}

ELEVEN-LINE STANZAS :

The triple Foole	a^6 a^8 b^6 b^{10} b^6 c d^{10} c^8 d e e^{10}
The Relique	a a b b^8 c^6 d^{10} d^6 c e e e^{10}
Lovers infinitenesse	a b^8 a b c d^{10} c d^8 e e^{10} e^8

TWELVE-LINE STANZAS :

Loves Alchymie
a a^{10} b^7 b a^{10} c^6 d^{10} d c^8 c e e^{10}

THIRTEEN-LINE STANZAS :

A Lecture upon the Shadow
a^8 a ^{10} bb^7 c d^{10} d^6 c^{10} e e^8 e f f^{10}

FOURTEEN-LINE STANZAS :

Aire and Angels
a b^8 b $a^{10}b^8$ a^{10} c^8 d^{10} c^8 $d^{10}d^8$ e_6 e e

Loves growth
a^{10} b a^6 b c c d e e d f f g g^{10}

NON-STANZAIC POEMS :

The Token
a b a b c d c d e f e f g h g h i i

The Apparition
a^{10} b^6 b^{10} a^8 b c d c^{10} d^4 c^8 e f
f^6 e g g g^{10}

Womans constancy
a^8 a b^{10} b^4 c c c d e e^{10} d^8 f f
g^{10} g^8 h^6 h^{10}

The Dissolution
a_6 b^8 c^{10} d^6 b_8 a c^{10} d^6 e^8 e^{10} f^6 fe 1
g^8 g^{10} h^6 h^8 i $i^{10}j^6$ k^4 k j^{10} j^{14}

The first fact that comes out is the extraordinary variety of metrical schemes in this slender collection of poems. Even Prof. Schipper's thoroughness has failed to record them all, since we cannot find the stanza of *The Sunne Rising* nor that of *Negative Love* in either of his works. If we leave out for the present the couplet pieces, on the one hand, and the nondescripts with which the list ends, on the other hand, there remain forty-nine distinctly stanzaic pieces, distributed among forty-six stanza-forms. No stanza-form is found in more than three pieces, and forty-four of them are found only in one piece each. Though the other portions of Donne's poetical work are very far from exhibiting the same variety as the *Songs and Sonets*, yet they offer instances of many forms that are not recorded in the table, which therefore must not be taken as exhausting the metrical resources of the poet.

This variety is achieved in three ways : changing,

from one piece to another, the number of the lines in each stanza, or the length of the individual lines, or the rhyme-scheme.

As regards the first means, it will be enough to point out that the *Art of English Poesie*, published in 1589 and commonly attributed to George Puttenham, describes « staves » of four, five, six, seven, eight, nine and ten « verses » (all of which are represented in the *Songs and Sonets* except the second sort), and then proceeds to say : « Of eleven and twelve I find none ordinary staves used in any vulgar language, neither doth it serve well to continue any historicall report and ballade, or other song : but is a dittie of it self, and no staffe, yet some moderne writers have used it but very seldome » (8). Even these shadowy precedents were, it seems, missing for stanzas of more than twelve lines, since Puttenham has not a word to say about them, even to forbid their use. And when Spenser, five years after the *Art of English Poesie* had appeared and at a time when Donne had already begun to write verse, attempted a stanza longer by half than the longest that had been known to Puttenham, he failed to conform all through his *Epithalamion* to the pattern he had chosen, but wavered between seventeen and nineteen lines. Though Donne never attempted anything quite so ambitious, the *Songs and Sonets* contain stanzas, not only of eleven and twelve, but also of thirteen and fourteen lines.

As regards the second means used to procure variety, there are to be found in the poems under consideration

---

(8) Arber's reprint, 1869, pp. 79-80.

lines of two, three, four, six, seven, eight, ten, twelve, and fourteen syllables. According to Puttenham the « shortest proportion [of meeter] is of foure sillables, and his longest of twelve, they that use it above, passe the bounds of good proportion ». Yet he soon contradicts himself in granting the name of « verse » to an isolated « foot » of two syllables provided it be used « in the first place, and midle, and end of a staffe », a fairly liberal rule. He delivers himself still more oracularly about the line of three syllables, and, though he « finde no savour » in it, allows it as well as the other « odde » lines, to « be used for varietie sake, and specially being enterlaced with others » (9). But when he comes to quote instances, we see that he means rather the use of an hypermetrical syllable at the end of the line than the initial truncation which results in Donne's trisyllabic and heptasyllabic lines. Puttenham cannot but be acquainted with « verses of foureteene sillables », having « the *Cesure* at the first eight », but to him that « proportion is tedious » (10). If Donne, then, did not innovate here, he used all the lengths of lines known to his contemporaries. And he did innovate in the way he combined the different metres in the same stanza. Out of forty-nine pieces, seven only are isometrical (including one in which the heptasyllabic is occasionally substituted for the octosyllabic) ; in eighteen, two measures are found ; in sixteen, three ; in eight, four. Which of his contemporaries has used so many metres in so many ways ?

As regards the third means of varying stanza-forms,

(9) *Ibid.*, p. 84.
(10) *Ibid.*, p. 86.

Donne's ability and success are less conspicuous. Puttenham had taught him, with the help of many diagrams,
that « scituation in concord », which we call the arrangement of rhymes, cannot be such that the poet should
please everybody : if the distance between lines that
rhyme is too wide, « the rude and popular eare » loses
the « concord » ; if there is no distance, or too short a
one, « the learned and delicate eare » is offended (11). In
the large majority of the *Songs and Sonets* Donne, out
of carelessness, it seems, will disappoint the fastidious
hearer, though it is doubtful whether he will satisfy the
plain man. He does not stick at stanzas consisting merely of couplets or triplets following one another : *aabb,
aabbcc, aabbccc, aabbccdd, aabbcccddd, aabbcccddd ;* that
of the *Anniversarie* even ends on four consecutive lines
rhyming together, after a succession of three couplets
Even when he takes a little more pains, he seldom goes
further than « the second distance » and « the third
distance », to use Puttenham's phrases, *i. e.* the crossed
rhyme and the enfolding rhyme, while Petrarch in his *Can-
zoni*, as the *Arte of English Poesie* reminds us, has gone
as far as « the twelfth distance » (12). Perhaps the only
noteworthy exception in the *Songs and Sonets* to this
habit of propinquity is to be found in *The Message:*

> Send home my harmlesse heart againe,
> Which no unworthy thought could staine ;
> But if it be taught by thine
> To make jestings
> Of protestings,
> And crosse both
> Word and oath,
> Keepe it, for then 'tis none of mine.

---

(11) *Ibid.*, p. 100.
(12) *Ibid.*, pp. 99-100.

Between the two *b* rhymes four lines intervene, but « they
be so little and short as they make no show of any great
delay », according to Puttenham's judicious observation (13).
One will also notice that, while the *b* rhymes enfold
both the *c* and *d* rhymes, the *a* rhymes, which are not to
be heard again (14), form an independent couplet at the
beginning of the stanza, not without damage to its unity.
Yet Donne might here justify himself by pointing out
that, at any rate in each of the first two stanzas of this
piece, the metrical break agrees well with the meaning,
and makes the lover's recantation of his command more
impressive : it looks as if he forsook both his amorous
intent and his metrical design. But I should offer this
explanation on Donne's behalf with more confidence if
it were not his common practice to open his stanzas in
this manner, even when the most favourable critic cannot account for his doing so. Of the ten-line stanza in *The
Progresse of the Soule* ($aabccbbdd^{10} d^{12}$) Professor Saintsbury says « it ruins itself from the outset by starting with
a couplet, the very worst preparation of the ear for the
distinctive rhyming which is to follow » (15). This remark, almost unmitigated, might apply to not a few of
the *Songs and Sonets*. Indeed it is only one count in a
charge which might be stated thus in general terms :
Donne's stanzas, while they do not divide according to
the medieval rules, nearly always lack internal concatenation or rhyme-linking. Most of his eight-line stanzas,

---

(13) *Ibid.*, p. 99.

(14) In the first stanza the *d* rhymes are in « ee » like the *a* rhymes, a
piece of carelessness which well might mislead the reader. The stanza
quoted above is the second.

(15) *Op. cit.*, II, 161-2.

for instance, fall into two quatrains : *abab* + *cdcd*, or *abab* + *cddc*, or even *abab* + *ccdd* (not to mention again such as consist wholly of parallel rhymes and may fall into two or four parts at will), an « error » against which Puttenham had warned him. Indeed this metrist, however awkwardly he expresses himself on the point, had recognized the necessity of « a band » to make « the staffe... fast and not loose ». More important than Puttenham's theory is Spenser's example in *The Faery Queene* : the Spenserian stanza cannot be broken up ; it is an indivisible whole (16). The same may be said of a very few of the forms instanced in the *Songs and Sonets* ; and among these few the quatrain with crossed rhymes, *abab*, is the simplest of the well-tried schemes which Donne condescended to use. The only other forms which have an unquestionable claim to metrical indivisibility are to be found in *The Prohibition*, *aabcbcaa*, and *The Canonization*, *abbacccaa*. But shall these alone pass muster ? Shall some forty of the stanza-forms here represented be condemned because they lack this kind of unity ?

Such a sweeping condemnation would show the danger of an uncorrected analytic method. Il is only on paper, and through the agency of figures and letters, or geometrical drawings like Puttenham's, that we can dissociate the three elements which go to the making of a stanza. The ear, which judges synthetically, remains the supreme court of appeal and will quash many a seemingly well-grounded sentence. Take *The Anniversarie*, which

---

(16) I do not use the word *indivisible* here in Schipper's sense. Indeed his indivisible stanzas really fall into two unconnected parts ; see *A History of English versification*, § 253.

offers the least promising of rhyme-schemes : *aabbccdddd ;*
the mere variation of metre communicates to it sufficient
lyrical impetus :

> All Kings, and all their favorites,
> All glory of honors, beauties, wits,
> The Sum it selfe, which makes times, as they passe,
> Is elder by a yeare, now, then it was
> When thou and I first one another saw :
> All other things, to their destruction draw,
> Only our love hath no decay ;
> This, no to morrow hath, nor yesterday,
> Running it never runs from us away,
> But truly keepes his first, last, everlasting day.

The staid decasyllabics twice receive the impulse of the
nimbler octosyllabics, while the final alexandrine, Spenser-
wise, adds a deeper resonance. And in other pieces,
so well-known that they need not be quoted here, Donne,
with little more assistance from the rhyme-scheme, leads
us through each strophe, never allowing us to rest until
we have returned to the metrical starting-point : witness
the two songs, equally swinging though written in such
different moods, « *Sweetest love, I do not goe* », and
« *Goe and catche a falling starre* ». What English lyric
ever excelled these in *élan* ?

However, this study is concerned not only with Donne's
achievements but with his attempts, whether success-
ful or not. It has already established his claim to metrical variety. Originality, though at once conjectured, is
not so easy to ascertain ; recourse must be had to reper-
tories such as Professor Schipper's, and even when no
earlier instance of a stanza is recorded by them, that is
no absolute proof that Donne invented it. With this reservation, the figures we arrive at still carry conviction.
Out of forty-six stanza-forms in the *Songs and Sonets*, on-

ly four, according to Schipper, are found before Donne used them, *viz* : the common measure, $a^8b^6a^8b^6$ (*The Undertaking*, <*Selfe Love*>) — the long measure, $abab^8$ (*A Feaver*, *A Valediction : forbidding mourning*, *The Extasie* — the quatrain of Marlowe's « *Come live with mee, and bee my love* », $aabb$ (*The Baite*) — and a sixain first found in the *Ægloga prima* of *The Shepheardes Calender*, but best-known as the stanza of *Venus and Adonis*, $ababcc^{10}$ (*The Expiration*). All the longer and more complex stanzas, it would seem, are of Donne's invention. But the exceptional character of the *Songs and Sonets* is still more vividly realized if we look not only before but after. Out of the forty-two stanza-forms which are not found earlier, Schipper gives later instances of three only, *viz* : an isometrical, four-foot line, variation of the *rime couée*, $aabccb^8$ (*Communitie*) which was used, among others, by Suckling (with a feminine *b* rhyme), — a sixain, $aabb^8cc^{10}$ (*Breake of day*), which Landor took up, — and an eight-line stanza, $a^{10}a^8bb^{10}cc^8dd^{10}$ (*The Dampe*), which Cowley copied. Of course it would be even rasher to assert that any one stanza of Donne's had no successors than to deny the possibility of its having had forgotten predecessors. But there remains the broad fact that most of the forms he used were used by nobody else (17). In this particular he may well be said to stand apart from the body of the English lyrists.

Adverse criticism might question, if not the extent, **at**

---

(17) This remark partly applies to the non-stanzaic pieces. See *infra* for *The Token*, *The Apparition*, *Womans constancy*, and *The Dissolution*. — On the other hand not only the isometrical couplet of *The Computation*, but also the anisometrical one of *A Paradox*, had been used before Donne ; Schipper points to an instance of the latter in Sidney, *Psalm XLI*.

least the worth of this originality : among the practically
unlimited number of possible stanzas many had never
been called to life because the poets foresaw that they
would be still-born ; Donne merely gave an *a posteriori*
demonstration of that truth; the more fool he ! — Puttenham gravely recommends this society game as a means
of asserting one's poetical powers : « Make me saith this
writer to one of the companie, so many strokes or lines
with your pen as ye would have your song containe
verses ; and let every line beare his severall length,
even as ye would have your verse of measure. Suppose
of foure, five, sixe or eight or more sillables, and set
a figure of everie number at th'end of the line, whereby
ye may know his measure. Then where you will have
your rime or concord to fall, marke it with a compast
stroke or semicircle passing over those lines.... And
bycause ye shall not thinke the maker hath premeditated
beforehand any such fashioned ditty, do ye your selfe
make one verse...., and give it him for a theame to
make all the rest upon : if ye shall perceive the maker
do keepe the measures and rime as ye have appointed
him, and besides do make his dittie sensible and ensuant
to the first verse in good reason, then may ye say he is
his crafts maister. » (18) Might not Donne's metrical pat-
terns have been forced upon him, regardless of beauty, as
puerile tests in versifying ?

Such criticism, however pungent, appears at once to
be unfair. An appreciation which saw nothing but artificiality in the *Songs and Sonets* would be even more
clearly at fault than a belief in their perfect earnestness.

---

(18) Arber's reprint, pp. 103-4.

Donne's use of stanza-forms was no mere dallying, and
their choice, whether well or ill advised, was emphatic-
ally his own. Besides, while Puttenham's poet is to write
only one « dittie » on each form proposed to him, the
most surprizing fact, metrically, about the *Songs and
Sonets*, is the fidelity with which the second and next
stanzas reproduce the first, however careless and hap-
hazard its design may seem. A glance through the above
table will show that most of them are difficult enough,
irrespective of the judgement passed upon their artistic
merit.

Before I proceed to draw inferences from this self-
imposed labour of Donne's, I must meet two objections
which the reader of the *Songs and Sonets* might make.
The first is that Donne now and then allows himself some
licence, not indeed as regards the number of lines and
order of rhymes, but in the matter of line-lengths. Here
is a list, an exhaustive one as I trust (19), of such anomalies. The text from which it has been compiled is that
of the 1633 edition, but in several lines later editions or
manuscripts provide the missing syllables or do away
with the supernumeraries :

The Indifferent, stanza III, line 3, has 14 syllables instead
of 12 (but 12 only in the 1635-69 edd.).

« *Sweetest love, I do not goe* », st. I, l. 6, has 6 syllables
instead of 7 in the four other stanzas (but 7 in 1635-54
edd.).

Aire and Angels, st. II, l. 5, has 10 syllables instead of 8.

A Valediction : of my name, in the window, st. III, l. 1,

---

(19) Except for the substitution of the heptasyllabic for the octosyllabic,
on which see *supra*, n. 7.

LIBRARY
OF
MOUNT ST. MARY'S
COLLEGE
EMMITSBURG, MARYLAND

has 7 syllables instead of 6 (but may be reduced to 6 by the elision of « thy » before « inconsiderate »).

Loves exchange, st. II and III, l. 4, and st. II, l. 7, have 8 syllables instead of 10.

Witchcraft by a picture, st. II, ll. 2 and 3, have 8 instead of 10 syllables, and l. 4 has 10 instead of 8.

The Primrose, st. II, l. 7, has 10 syllables instead of 8 (but 8 only in 1635-9 edd. and several mss.).

<*Selfe Love*>, st. III, l. 4, has 7 syllables instead of 6.

It will no doubt be granted that, notwithstanding those few metrical deviations, Donne is entitled to the praise of exactness which I have bestowed upon him : over forty of the *Songs and Sonets*, including most of those where the stanza-form offers the greatest difficulties, show perfect regularity throughout.

But then comes the second objection : the number of stanzas in each piece is in the inverse ratio to the length and complexity of the stanza-form ; or to put it less pedantically, the more intricate the pattern, the fewer the copies. *The Extasie* runs to nineteen quatrains, and *A Valediction: of my name, in the window*, to eleven sixains; while the fourteen-line stanza-forms of *Aire and Angels* and *Loves growth*, the thirteen-line form of *A Lecture upon the Shadow*, the twelve-line form of *Loves Alchymie*, the eleven-line form of *The triple Foole* are repeated but once, and the eleven-line forms of *The Relique* and *Lovers infiniteness*, but twice. Yet even this is no mean achievement, or at least no small tour de force. Besides, Donne gives no less than four stanzas in the ten-line form of *Farewell to love*, and from five to seven of each of the nine-line forms in *A nocturnall*, *The Canonization*, *The Will*, and *A Valediction : of the booke*. Il any

one feels inclined to minimize this feat by recalling the four
thousand stanzas in *The Faery Queene* (which death only
prevented from being double that number), the answer
is that the Spenserian stanza, though more beautiful than
any of those that Donne devised, consists only of decasyllabics and a final alexandrine, and therefore does not
equal them in their characteristic difficulty : the variation
of line-lengths. Moreover, that Donne could hammer
again and again the same stanza-form, however bulky
(and faulty at that), his *Progresse of the Soule* sufficiently
testifies ; when he stopped at the end of the fifty-first
specimen of it, he was rather disgusted with his theme
than tired with his metre.

But mere number matters little : for my purpose it is
enough that Donne should have reproduced once at least
each of the forms tabulated above, except four. Of these
four, which have so far been left out of reckoning, *The
Token* offers only that interest of adding one more experiment to the metrical variety of the *Songs and Sonets* ;
in point of originality, though it seems to be unique of
its kind, at any rate in English poetry (Schipper does not
even record it), it differs from the Shakespearian sonnet
only by the insertion of a fourth quatrain before the final
couplet ; it is merely one of many abortive attempts at
creating new species of an extremely popular genus. Not
so with the three other pieces, *Womans constancy*, *The
Apparition*, and *The Dissolution*. Here Donne is breaking
new ground, on which many a future crop will be raised.
Any rule or order as regards metre or rhyme is disregarded ; verse could not be freer, it seems, without losing
the name of verse. The effect thus produced, especially in
The Apparition, is striking. As few anthologists or critics

have ever quoted this piece (20) (nor the two others,
it seems), I give it here in full :

> When by thy scorne, O murdresse, I am dead,
>   And that thou thinkst thee free
> From all solicitation from mee,
> Then shall my ghost come to thy bed,
> And thee, fain'd vestall, in worse armes shall see,
> Then thy sicke taper will begin to winke,
> And he, whose thou art then, being tyr'd before,
> Will, if thou stirre, or pinch to wake him thinke
>   Thou call'st for more.
> And in false sleepe will from thee shrinke,
> And then poore Aspen wretch, neglected thou
> Bath'd in a cold quicksilver sweat wilt lye
>   A veryer ghost then I ;
> What I will say, I will not tell thee now,
> Lest that preserve thee' ; and since my love is spent,
> I'had rather thou shouldst painfully repent,
> Then by my threatnings rest still innocent.

Donne never wrote anything stronger than *The Apparition*, and one could well contend that the strict economy
of words ensured by the close-fitting metrical garment is
the chief secret of its strength. Any syllable added any-
where, *metri gratia*, would make it less tense ; hate vould
become somewhat verbose, instead of uttering itself with
unsurpassed conciseness. Neither *Womans constancy* nor
The Dissolution come up to the same height of eloquence,
but the former equals and the latter exceeds *The Apparition* in metrical freedom : this contains lines of four, six,
eight, and ten syllables : *The Dissolution* has all those, and
besides it ends on a fourteener ; as regards rhyme it uses
not only the third, but even the fourth and fifth « dis-
tances ». It will not be left very far behind even by George

---

(20) The motives of this neglect appear to be rather moral than metrical.
See H. J. Massingham, *A treasury of seventeenth century English verse*,
p. 334.

Herbert in *The Collar*, perhaps the most characteristic specimen of English free verse in a very short compass.

Now, if the theory of Donne's absolute intellectual and sentimental earnestness were adequate, what fitter medium could he find than that, and, having once found it, how could he use any other ? If a poem ran to such length as to make divisions necessary, why did he not use the pseudo-pindaric strophes ? What Cowley did invent, his master might easily have invented. The significant fact is that Donne never wrote any such ode, and that he wrote no more than three pieces in free verse. The second best medium for an overactive brain and eruptive heart would have been such simple, familiar metres as the common or the long measures, because they interfere little with thought and feeling ; those metres Donne did use in some of his best pieces, e. g. *The undertaking* and *The Extasie ;* yet they are not prevalent, any more than free verse, in the *Songs and Sonets.* A theory, therefore, which cannot account for the large majority of Donne's lyrical pieces, including such fine ones as *The Sunne Rising, The Dreame, The Anniversarie, The Relique, Lovers infiniteness, Aire and Angels,* to quote only those which are written in the most complex stanzas, — that theory ought to be rejected, if only because of its failure to stand the metrical test.

A dualistic explanation of Donne's practice seems to me necessary here. In such pieces as *The Apparition*, but also in the first stanza of most of the *Songs and Sonets*, thought and feeling are allowed to shape their metrical mould, unhampered by any convention or tradition. In the following stanzas the position is completely reversed : thought and feeling are at great pains to fit themselves into the now hardened mould. In other words, the extreme of freedom becomes the extreme of slavery. Let us take for instance *Loves Alchymie :*

> Some that have deeper digg'd loves Myne then I,
> Say, where his centrique happinesse doth lie :
> I have lov'd, and got, and told,
> But should I love, get, tell, till I were old
> I should not finde that hidden mysterie ;
> Oh, 'tis imposture all :
> And as no chymique yet th' Elixar got.
> But glorifies his pregnant pot,
> If by the way to him befall
> Some odoriferous thing, or medicinall,
> So lovers dreame a rich and long delight,
> But get a winter-seeming summer night.

Between these twelve lines and the seventeen lines of *The Apparition*, there is no more than a numerical difference ; the same subordination of form to matter obtains throughout both metrical units. Indeed we cannot call the above-quoted stanza anything but free verse until we see it repeated with the most minute accuracy :

> Our ease, our thrift, our nonor, and our day,
> Shall we, for this vaine Bubles shadow pay ?
> Ends love in this, that my man,
> Can be as happy'as I can ; If he can
> Endure the short scorne of a Bridegroomes play ?
> That loving wretch that sweares,
> 'Tis not the bodies manry, but the mindes,
> Which he in her Angelique findes,
> Would sweare as justly, that he heares,
> In that dayes rude hoarse minstralsey, the spheares.
> Hope not for minde in women, at their best
> Sweetnesse and wit, they'are but *Mummy*, possest.

The skill of the versifier will get its meed of praise ; he may well be styled, in Puttenham's phrase, « his crafts maister ». Yet no reader but will feel how differently the two stanzas ring ; the former is, metrically speaking, a

« rather irresponsible experiment » (21) ; the latter is a cleverly executed task. While its closing couplet hits harder and straighter from the shoulder than any individual line in the original « ditty », the copy lacks that flow, or swing, which resulted from carelesness, I mean, unconcern. It is more discursive, and less spirited.

Is *Loves Alchymie* typical in this respect ? To answer this question with perfect confidence one should discuss the comparative merits of stanzas in each of the *Songs and Sonets*, or at least in all which are written neither in free verse nor in short and easy metrical forms. Moreover, in such a purely aesthetic problem the critic should not lay down a law which would be no more than the dogmatic expression of his personal preference. I shall therefore confine myself to pointing out that in such a match, *the first stanza v. the rest*, the odds are on the side of the first stanza. At any rate we must prognosticate its superiority if we assume that it flowed from Donne's pen as the spontaneous outpouring of his soul. But the opposite assumption also suggests itself, to wit that the poet conceived his pattern in the abstract, perhaps with the help of diagrams like Puttenham's, and then the first stanza may be, not the original, but a copy of that « idea », as a Platonist would say ; it may be, the chances even are that it should be, a clumsy copy, the work of an inexpert hand. According to such a view, and since practice makes perfect, the later stanza should generally show more ease and skill than the preceding one. *Farewell to love* might be adduced as evidence :

---

(21) This phrase is Professor Saintsbury's, *op. cit.*, II, p. 165 ; he applies it chiefly, it seems, to the internal structure of the lines.

> Whilst yet to prove,
> I thought there was some Deitie in love,
> So did I reverence, and gave
> Worship ; as Atheists at their dying houre
> Call, what they cannot name, an unknowne power,
> As ignorantly did I crave .
> Thus when
> Things not yet knowne are coveted by men,
> Our desires give them fashion, and so
> As they waxe lesser, fall, as they sise, grow.

Though the whole stanza consists of one period, one can hardly call it a success. It is cumbered with ill-adjusted clauses (are the two *as* of lines 4 and 6 correlative or independent ? is the former *as* correlative with *so* in line 3 ?). On the contrary the second stanza, in spite of a break in the sense at the end of the fifth line, achieves sufficient unity, and reads off easily, I should say pleasantly if it were not for the sadness of its lesson :

> But, from late faire
> His highnesse sitting in a golden Chaire,
> Is not lesse cared for after three dayes
> By children, then the thing which lovers so
> Blindly admire, and with such worship wooe ;
> Being had, enjoying it decayes :
> And thence,
> What before pleas'd them all, takes but one sense,
> And that so lamely, as it leaves behinde
> A kinde of sorrowing dulnesse to the minde.

Unfortunately the third and fourth stanzas fall off from the standard of metrical exellence established by the second. But in *A Valediction : of weeping* the last stanza is incomparably the most beautiful. Whether we adopt Chambers's or Grierson's punctuations (both conjectural), the opening stanza seems awkward with its reduplication of the conjunction *for* (ll. 3 and 5), and the asyndeton of ll. 7-8 which leaves the connexion of ideas very much in doubt. The second stanza consists of one sentence and

flows well to the end of the seventh line ; but the additional clause in the last two lines may be said to upset its
balance ; and, even if it were perfect metrically, the over-
ingeniousness of the comparison between the poet's tear
« impressed » with the image of his mistress and the
« round ball » on which a cartographer copies the various
parts of the world would prevent the reader from being
swept away in the whirlwind of passion. This is why
critics usually quote the third stanza alone : « O more then
Moone, — Draw not up seas to drowne me in thy
spheare..... » is as familiar to the English public as any of
Donne's « fine onsets », to use Mrs. Meynell's apt phrase.
Yet one might contend that the last stanza depends for its
full effect upon the rather laborious conceits of the first
two, and that separating it from them exposes it to the
risk of being imperfectly understood. In this piece,
therefore, Donne appears to have warmed himself up pro-
gressively. One of his most pathetic movements, perhaps
his most triumphant vindication of hyperbole as the language of passion, owes at least something to acquired
mastery, to craftsmanship, to artistic endeavour.

It remains that *A Valediction : of weeping* can hardly be paralleled in this respect by any other lyric of
Donne's. In many, if not most, of the *Songs and Sonets*, an
initial outburst of feeling soon subsides into dialectics,
a change which I ascribe to the difficulty of reproducing
deliberately the complex arrangement of a spontaneous
first stanza. In such pieces one may admire Donne's art
less than in the above, one may even deplore it ; yet one
should acknowledge its presence, and its importance to
the poet. His having tried free verse makes his preference
for those stanzaic forms which may be said to break the

back of his inspiration all the more characteristic. Indeed free verse, as La Fontaine's fables evidence, admits of supreme artistic excellence, but it is also, and more frequently, resorted to by writers who think their matter poetic enough to dispense with obvious metrical adornment. Donne's poetry does not choose to go thus naked. The metrical variety and originality it wants to achieve must be something tangible, numerical rather than numerous. It parades its freedom from tradition up to a certain point chiefly to enhance the value of its strict subjection afterwards to its own new-made laws. When it seems to have given itself most rope, it proves to have tied itself tightest.

*
* *

Whatever view of the relation between the metrical mould and the poetical matter poured therein the reader may adopt, he can hardly deny that Donne paid no less attention to the mould than to the matter. But what has just been called matter in contradistinction to metrical form is no raw material ; it has already passed through a process of elaboration. To show this more clearly, let us leave the *Songs and Sonets* for a while, and go to Donne's prose letters.

Here, for instance, is one to the Countess of Bedford (also the addressee of several verse-letters and perhaps of some lyrical pieces), which begins : « Madam, — Amongst many other dignities..... » (22). The occasion of it is this : Lord Harrington, the Countess's brother, has told her that Donne has written, which is contrary to fact. Donne,

---

(22) Gosse, *Life and letters of John Donne*, II, 42.

who has evidently nothing to say, now sets out to indite
the letter which he is supposed to have written already.
His fertile brain finds in this trifling accident occasion for
a number of conceits. The letter, he says, was « pro-
phesied of before it was born ». Harrington showed great
confidence in Donne when he called what was still a mere
promise « an act already done ». In return Donne does
Harrington a service by making good that passage of
Harrington's letter which said that the poet had written.
If Donne should not write, he would be twice guilty,
first in neglecting Lady Bedford and secondly in making
Harrington lie to his sister. But in order that the Countess should accept this apology, it remains to explain
away the discrepancy between the imaginary and the actual dates of the letter. Here Donne uses his scholastic
knowledge to good effect : what is time ? a mere civil or-
dinance, important only in wills or birthrights ; but souls
participate of the divine nature which sees all things in
one eternal present. The letter, being an act of pure friendship, nay love, is exempt from « straitness of hours ».
Lady Bedford could hardly be angry at the delay which
lent itself to such elaborate apologies. She would probably
have put up with much more such badinage, and Donne
was well able to carry it on much longer ; we moderns
ought then to be thankful to him that he did not. Yet,
while we prefer Madame de Sévigné's letters to Voiture's,
we must confess that the amount of art in Voiture's is
greater : similarly Donne the letter-writer must be granted
the merit, such as it is, of making something out of nothing. He could fill two sides of a sheet without com-
municating the smallest item of news or uttering the least
genuine feeling. If that is not craftsmanship, what is ?

When he became a preacher he did not banish subtlety but transplanted it. He was not indeed the first nor the last, to speak for an hour, nay hours, on the most barren verse of Scripture, distorting the plainest words to give them one, two or more symbolical meanings. I do not venture to say that he outdid all his colleagues in this art but he certainly went very far. Is it then to be expected that, except for occasional concessions to metrical necessities, we should find in the *Songs and Sonets* the language of the heart ? It is far more likely that hair-splitting, practised for its own sake, should often prevail.

Of this perverse wit the notorious *Flea* is an extreme example, and it would be unfair to judge all the lyrical poetry of Donne by it. Yet the theme of many pieces, while it is less ludicrous, is not less slight, and hyperbole in the manner appears as the almost inevitable counterpart of insignificance in the matter. In actual height of hyperbole it was next to impossible to outbid the Petrarchists ; but their worst fault was not extravagance, it was monotony. Donne at any rate avoids this. Even when he takes up the hackneyed metaphors of love-fires, sigh-tempests, and tear-floods, he words them out in an unexpected manner. To support this assertion it will suffice to refer the reader to the analysis of *A Valediction : of weeping*, given above. Hardly less worn out in Donne's time was the comparison of the loved one to a heathen goddess, or even to a Christian saint or angel. While the almost complete absence of mythology from his poetry, as his disciple Carew was to note, is perhaps the most striking difference betewen him and his contemporaries, he turned to account in his most

profane writings a knowledge of scholastic theology un-
equalled by any English poet before or since. In *The
Dreame* he confesses to his mistress that on her coming
into the room he mistook her for a mere angel ; but
when he saw that she knew his thoughts by direct intui-
tion, he realized that he had been guilty of blasphemy,
since that power is denied to the celestial hierarchy and
she shares it with God alone (23). The rejuvenation of a
decrepit hyperbole will generally be acknowledged here,
but to what elixir will it be ascribed ? Passion there undoubtedly is in this piece, and hyperbole, as we have
noted, sometimes expresses real passion ; but the love
of the poet for his mistress is cheerfully sensual, without any admixture of genuine reverence, so that the
high-flown compliment sounds insincere, or at least
sportive and witty rather than passionate. More of this
anon ; let us grant that in *The Canonization, The Funerall*, and *The Relique*, there is no such discrepancy between the religious metaphors and the amorous feelings ;
we have said enough for the present to show that hyperbole in the *Songs and Sonets*, whether traditional or
original, has more to do with art than is allowed by the
theory of Donne's volcanic self-utterance.

Not hyperbole however but the « closely knit logical
structure » (24) of each piece is the chief characteristic of
his lyrical poetry, considered from the rhetorician's point
of view. There are few of the *Songs and Sonets* where
an almost syllogistic concatenation of thought does not

---

(23) See Grierson's note on ll. 15-16 of this piece.
(24) The phrase is Professor Grierson's, in his *Metaphysical lyrics and
poems of the seventeenth century*, p. 223, apropos of Carew. See also pp.
XXXIV-XXXV.

appear, if not at once, yet to him who takes sufficient pains.

Communitie is a trifle ; that by the law of nature all women belong to every man was a stock theme with the ancient sceptics and epicureans, and in the middle ages it could even boast the sanction of the gravest divines, under whose patronage Jean de Meun sheltered himself when his mouthpiece the Old Dame expressed it, together with the converse proposition, in the plainest terms : Nature, she says,

> nous a faiz, beaus fiz, n'en doutes,
> Toutes pour touz et touz pour toutes,
> Chascune pour chascun comune,
> Et chascun comun a chascune (25).

Donne is no less outspoken though he is more elliptical : in his « All, all may use », the first « all » is probably the object and the second the subject of the verb, but the question is purely grammatical, since in explicit prose it certainly means that all men may enjoy all women. This is the doctrine of free love in its crudest form, and the poet does not take it quite seriously, though (or shall we say because ?) his practice at the time probably conformed to it. But the crudity and staleness of the thought only make the originality of the expression more apparent. Sensual appetite here parades in a cap and gown, fresh from the Universities or the Inns of Court. The major proposition is unimpeachable, so as to catch the confidence of the most orthodox :

---

(25) *Le Roman de la Rose*, ll. 13885-8 in Langlois' edition. — Quoted by Louis I. Bredvold, *The Naturalism of Donne in Relation to Some Renaissance Traditions* (*Journal of English and Germanic Philology*, Oct. 1923, XXII, 489), from whom I also borrow the information concerning the previous fortunes of that theory.

> Good wee must love, and must hate ill,
> For ill is ill, and good good still.

Who would not feel safe on hearing such a truism ? Who would not allow the modest reservation :

> But there are things indifferent,
> Which wee may neither hate nor love,
> But one, and then another prove,
> As wee shall finde our fancy bent.

Even the word fancy, so slily introduced, does not startle the reader at once, with such respectability has the whole stanza been invested by the opening couplet. The second stanza particularizes ; it consists of two well-balanced halves, the former presenting an absurd hypothesis :

> If then at first wise Nature had
> Made women either good or bad,
> Then some wee might hate, and some chuse,

the latter substituting for it a sober fact :

> But since shee did them so create,
> That we may neither love nor hate,

and its logical consequence :

> Onely this rests, All, all may use.

The innocent reader feels a shock ; he cannot accept such a conclusion ; then something must be wrong with the premisses, but what ? Donne does not allow him time to find out for himself ; in the quietest manner he sets to support his contention that women are neither good nor bad :

> If they were good it would be seene,
> Good is as visible as greene,
> And to all eyes it selfe betrayes :
> If they were bad, they could not last,
> Bad doth it selfe and others wast,
> So, they deserve nor blame, nor praise.

This looks so impartial and dispassionate that the reader

whose attention has been drawn off from the scandalous
practical advice may well be tempted to grant something
like an assent to the third stanza. While thus staggered
he receives the straight hit of the fourth :

> But they are ours as fruits are ours,
> He that but tasts, he that devours,
> And he that leaves all, doth as well.

Note that the third line justifies even continence. Such
broad-mindedness evinces the intellectual superiority of
one who is not pleading his own case, not justifying his
own sensual wildness, but speaking the whole truth. The
last three lines however, plain-spoken to the point of cynicism, are probably meant to dispel the perplexity created
by the foregoing arguments :

> Chang'd loves are but chang'd sorts of meat,
> And when hee hath the kernell eate,
> Who doth not fling away the shell ?

Yet even here the poet uses his reasoning powers ; his
parting shot, if one may say so, is a final corollary, expressed in a homely metaphor ; there is no suspicious
appeal to the senses or to the imagination, but a far
more effective reducing of an all-important duty to insignificance.

In *Communitie* Donne perplexes his reader without
himself feeling the least hesitation about the conclusion
at which he will arrive. More frequently however he
seems to discuss a moot point with himself. He raises
objections and then tries to refute them, or he shifts his
position from stanza to stanza. The structure of that fine
lyric, *The Prohibition*, belongs to the balanced type : the
first stanza contains the thesis, the second the antithesis,

and the third the synthesis. The demonstration of thesis
and antithesis is carried on strictly parallel lines :

Take heed of loving mee .... (St. I, 1. 1)
Take heed of hating mee .... (St. II, 1. 1)
Not that I shall repaire .... (St. I, 1. 3)
Not that I shall be .... (St. II, 1. 3)
But .... (St. I, 1. 6)
But .... (St. II, 1. 5)
Then, least thy love, by my death, frustrate bee,
If thou love mee, take heed of loving mee. (St. I, 11. 7-8)
Then, least my being nothing lessen thee,
If thou hate mee, take heed of hating mee. (St. II, 11. 7-8)

The third stanza falls into two parts, of four lines each,
which are also built symmetrically ; to the *yet* of the
first line corresponds the *or* of the fifth, and the con-
sequences expressed in the second and sixth are both introduced by *so*. Within the first part of the stanza, lines
three and four balance each other in such a way as to
recall the opposition of the first two stanzas :

Love mee, that I may die the gentler way ;
Hate mee, because thy love is too great for mee ;

and the final couplet twice again opposes the two feelings
and the two words :

Lest thou thy love and hate and mee undoe,
To let mee live, O love and hate mee too.

Now the thought in this piece is paradoxical, but not
necessarily original ; the feeling, that doubtfulness of
the lover who does not know whether he wishes to see
his love returned, may or may not have been experienced
in actual life by the poet ; but both thought and feeling
have undergone a highly artistic, not to say artificial,
elaboration, and form is paramount here, as it will be
in Carew's *Mediocrity in love rejected*, a piece whose
theme and handling somewhat resemble those of *The*

Prohibition, but which seems to have had another, possibly a French, original (26).

In *The Message* each of the first two stanzas begins with an order or wish (contained in a couplet, as I have pointed out above), which the other six lines proceed to revoke ; the parallelism between those two stanzas is almost as perfect as in *The Prohibition*, and the last stanza also reconciles the contradictions so sharply drawn before ; the cancelled wishes are reiterated, and justified in an unexpected way. That Donne met more than once with the type of coquette whom he addresses here, appears most likely ; if so, he no doubt felt the anger expressed in his verse ; the cruelty of the hope that his mistress will « languish — For some one — That will none, — Or prove as false as she is now », looks genuine. Yet the careful balancing of its parts remains the most noticeable feature of this piece, as of the preceding one, which it equals in lyrical beauty.

The structure of *A Lecture upon the Shadow* is bipartite, not tripartite: the poet expresses two related truths, or two opposite aspects of the same truth in two symmetrical stanzas. At least, so it seems at first sight. Yet this apparent simplicity hides more real complexity than *The Prohibition* or *The Message*, owing to a conflict between the idea and the symbol chosen to represent it. Donne uses metaphorical logic almost to the end, but

---

(26) See the note in Vincent's edition of Carew (*The Muses library*), which points to the resemblance between *Mediocrity in love rejected* and a piece of Lovelace's entitled *A la Bourbon*, with this text : « Done moy plus de pitié ou plus de creaulté [*sic*], car sans ce Je ne puis pas Vivre, ne morir ». Wilkinson, in his edition of Lovelace, I, 72, gives no information as regards the provenance of this French, which is not bad prose. It is therefore impossible to establish the relation between it and Donne's *The Prohibition*, if there is any.

suddenly discards it because his sense of reality will not yield even to his taste for regularity in structure. The first stanza compares the growth of love to the ascent of the sun during the forenoon, a comparison which is probably as old as poetry itself, but here recovers some freshness because the measure of the sun's height is taken indirectly, as on the dial, by the length of lovers' shadows :

> Stand still, and I will read to thee
> A Lecture, Love, in loves philosophy.
>   These three houres that we have spent,
>   Walking here, Two shadowes went
> Along with us, which we our selves produc'd ;
> But, now the Sunne is just above our head,
>   We doe those shadowes tread ;
>   And to brave clearnesse all things are reduc'd.
> So whilst our infant loves di grow,
> Disguises did, and shadowes, flow,
> From us, and our cares ; but now 'tis not so.

The moral is stated, without the help of metaphor, in a couplet which the 17th century printers, if not Donne himself, separated from the stanza — to which it really belongs — by a blank, in order to emphasize its gnomic quality :

> That love hath not attain'd the high'st degree,
> Which is still diligent lest others see.

While the first stanza states an actual experience and draws a lesson from it, the second foretells the future. Since the growth of love obeys the same laws as that of sunlight, its decay must come in the same gradual manner in which night takes the place of day :

> Except our loves at this noone stay,
> We shall new shadowes make the other way.
>   As the first were made to blinde
>   Others ; these which come behinde

Will worke upon our selves, and blind our eyes.
If our loves faint, and westwardly decline ;
   To me thou, falsly, thine,
   And I to thee mine actions shall disguise.
The morning shadowes weare away,
But these grow longer all the day.

So far the poet allows himself to be ruled by the metaphor. Now comes the revolt :

But oh, loves day is short, if love decay.

The fact that two successive lines begin with *but* may well puzzle the reader, and the lightness of the punctuation (a comma after *day*) may prevent him from seeing at once the full value of the second conjunction. It recognizes that he similitude does not hold good, for at least that it is imperfect (27). The final couplet, again detached typographically, manages to give a definition of love which is in accordance with fact and yet imaginatively related to the foregoing metaphor. Here poet and logician combine ; love belongs to the genus light, but it has a specific difference, a characteristic which distinguishes it from other kinds, *e. g.*, sunlight :

Love is a growing, or full constant light ;
And his first minute, after noone, is night.

The piece achieves unity after all, but there is no complete coincidence between metrical structure and reasoning process. Thought and craftsmanship collide in a way which is more interesting than satisfactory.

In *Lovers infiniteness* and *Loves Deitie* symmetry is restricted to the use of a metrical burden. In the former

(27) « No simile squares (*nihil simile est idem*) », as Coleridge remarks upon ll. 15-18 of *The good-morrow* (note written in Mr. Gillman's copy of *Chalmers' Poets* and dated Jenuary 1829).

piece every stanza ends on the word « all »; after perplexing the reader with subtle distinctions and objections couched in legal phraseology, the poet calls him back in unmistakable terms to the idea of totality, of entire self-surrender in love. Not without reason do some of the manuscripts change the English title to the French one of *Mon Tout*. From the point of view of art, hovewer, the piece is unpleasantly cumbered with *ifs*, and *yets*, and *thens*, which have different meanings, and seem to be correlated but are not. In spite of some beautiful lines I cannot agree with the anthologists which place it among the finest of the *Songs and Sonets*, and I much prefer *Loves Deitie*. The fate of this lyric is both curious and characteristic ; the first two lines, which appeal to the imagination, are quoted as often as anything else in Donne :

> I long to talke with some old lovers ghost,
> Who dyed before the god of Love was borne.

But there the success ends. The reader's disappointment at the following anticlimax :

> I cannot thinke that hee, who then lov'd most,
> Sunke so low, as to love one which did scorne,

reveals itself in the way the rest of the stanza and the following ones are ignored. Yet Signor Praz has shown excellently that the contrast between the traditionally poetical and the normally prosaic is the very essence of Donne's poetry (28). The Italian critic's analysis of *Loves Deitie* goes to the root of the matter, and it will suffice here to call attention to the visible unity which is

---

(28) *Secentismo...*, pp. 97-98.

provided by the repetition, in the last line of every stanza, of the words *love* (twice or thrice in each line), *her* or *she*, and *mee*, stressed, which provides the rhyme. Out of twenty-eight lines, sixteen thus rhyme together. As regards logical connexion, the first three stanzas develop the same thought : no one should love without being loved, and yet one does ; the fourth stanza does not indeed reconcile these contradictóy terms, what is and what should be ; but it reveals more vital truths by the side of which the former complaint sinks into insignificance :

> Rebell and Atheist too, why murmure I,
> As though I felt the worst that love could doe?
> Love might make me leave loving, or might trie
> A deeper plague, to make her love mee too,
> Which, since she loves before, I'am loth to see ;
> Falshood is worse then hate ; and that must bee,
> If shee whom I love, should love mee.

Opinions will differ as to the seriousness of the thought expressed in this stanza. The brusque exclamation with which it begins belongs to Donne's most impassioned manner. But like the evocation of the ghost in the first stanza it gives place at once to dialectics, rather ingenious than convincing, as it seems to me. The poet knows he must end on a statement similar in form, though directly opposite in meaning, to the concluding statements of the preceding stanza, and I chiefly admire the cleverness with which he manages to fit all the logical joints into the last three lines.

Many more instances of such cleverness might be adduced from the *Songs and Sonets*, but I have said enough to prove that Donne pays great attention to the working up of ideas, that there is a close relation between the artistic structure and the logical import of his lyrics, and that form not seldom seems to command matter. Yet one might object that such form is logical rather than artistic, and contend that Donne is more of a schoolman than a poet when he delights in symmetrical constructions, even to the making of blind windows. To refute this contention, I now mean to show that, in several at least of the *Songs and Sonets*, logic is subordinate to another element which I shall call the dramatic.

That Donne possessed dramatic power has generally been acknowledged (29). Indeed one of the generation which came to manhood in the last decade of the XVIth century might be credited with some measure of the instinct at work in Shakespeare and so many lesser playwrights, even before he had given evidence of it. In his fervid youth Donne was « a great Frequenter of Plays » (29 *bis*), though the theatres probably found in him a hard patron to please ; and even in his sermons

(29) Edward Dowden, *New studies in literature* (1895), p. 103, goes near to denying it : « Touches of dramatic power are rare in Donne, whose genius was lyrical and meditative, not that of a dramatist ; but in this Elegy [*By our first strange and fatall interview...*] there is one touch which might seem of triumphant power even if it had occurred in a tragedy of Webster ». The remark applies to ll. 50-54 : when I am gone on my continental journey, the lover says to his mistress, do not

in bed fright thy Nurse
With midnights startings, crying out, oh oh,
Nurse, ô my love is slaine, I saw him goe
O'r the white Alpes alone ; I saw him I,
Assail'd, fight, taken, stabb'd, bleed, fall and die.

The passage is very beautiful and moving but it is not strictly dramatic since the lover merely conjures up a vision of the future as in *The Apparition* (see *infra*).

(29 *bis*) Sir Richard Baker, *Chronicle of the Kings of England* (1730, p. 424) quoted in Grierson, II, 172. — Grierson also quotes a verse letter, addressed to Donne *c.* 1600 by « Willam Cornwaleys », which contains the lines :

If then for change of howers you seem careles,
Agree with me to lose them at the playes.

he will not boggle at comparisons drawn from play-acting (30).

Still that general agreement upon the epithet « dramatic » rather tends to confusion than enlightenment because no two critics seem to understand it in the same sense, and it may well be applied to Donne's poetry in more than one. If by « dramatic » you mean what stirs the emotions through the sight, especially, of attitudes and gestures, *The Apparition* will answer that definition best of all the *Songs and Sonets*. Here we have a sordid but striking *mise-en-scène* : the lovers in bed, the man pretending to sleep, the woman pinching him in vain, the « sicke taper » which begins « to winke » at the entrance of the ghost. Yet there is no touch of the melodrama in *The Apparition*, as there is in those pictures of Greuze that Diderot admired so much for their emotional

---

(30) « ...those transitory and interlocutory prayers, which out of custome and fashion we make, and still proceed in our sin ; when we pretend to speake to God, but like Comedians upon a stage, turne over our shoulder, and whisper to the Devill... » (*Donne's sermons, Selected passages...* by Logan Pearsall Smith, Oxford, 1920, p. 123).
There are several theatrical metaphors or comparisons in the poems :.

Men of France...
....the rightest company
Of Players, which upon the worlds stage be,
      (*Elegie XVI, On his Mistris*, ll. 33-36).
And Courts are Theaters, where some men play
Princes, some slaves..
      (*To Sr Henry Wotton* (Grierson, I, 181), ll. 23-24).
Beleeve me Sir, in my youths giddiest dayes,
When to be like the Court, was a playes praise,
Playes were not so like Courts, as Courts'are like playes.
      (*To Sr Henry Wotton* (Grierson. I, 188), ll. 19-21).
This is my playes last scene, here heavens appoint
My pilgrimages last mile...
      (*Holy Sonnets*, VI (Grierson, I, 324), ll. 1-2).
Evelyn M. Simpson, *A Study of the Prose Works of John Donne*, Oxford, 1924, pp. 61-62, says that in later life « he denounced comedies, wine and women as « Job's miserable comforters » to the down-cast soul ». Yet, she adds, « his friendship with Ben Jonson shows that he did not dislike the serious drama, while in his sermons he took up the position, in contrast to the Puritans, of a champion of all innocent amusements ».

intensity and that we cannot help smiling at to-day, *La Malédiction paternelle* and *Le fils puni*. But, with a difference in quality, there is the same method, the same composition. Such art is less akin to the drama than to the *tableau vivant*, be it said without a sneer. Action there is none ; the poet even refuses to tell his false mistress now what his ghost will say to her then, an artifice which reminds us of Timanthes hiding Agamemnon's face in his picture of Iphigenia's sacrifice. As the extreme of pity, so the extreme of terror is produced by suppression rather than expression.

Directly opposed to this pictorial conception of the dramatic is the purely psychological one. Mr. Massingham, for instance, thus praises, apropos of *The Relique*, the fitness of the style in the *Songs and Sonets* : « It is impossible to conceive those tremendous adventures of soul, mind and sense expressed by dainty, tripping lines, by smooth, ambling lines or even by the majestic sounding-board line of Milton, which expresses the reposeful sweep of the mind rather than its dramatic stress and conflict » (31). This amounts to saying that the soul of Donne in his lyrics divides against itself as, for instance, that of Othello in Shakespeare's play. But owing to the assumed identity of author and character, this is just a roundabout way of stating the theory of the poet's unqualified earnestness. Art, if it exists at all in the eyes of such criticism, is strictly subordinate to thought and feeling, feeling instinct with thought, or thought quickened by feeling.

---

(31) *Op. cit.*, p. 335.

I shall take the word dramatic in a third sense (32) :
in many of the *Songs and Sonets* there are two characters ;
the second is indeed a mute ; or rather his words are
not written down ; but we are enabled to guess how he
acts and what he would say if he were granted utterance. The way in which Donne gives us those hints is
both very clever and very modern. More important still
from the point of view adopted in this essay is the effect
produced on the speaking character by the presence of a
listening one, whom he tries to persuade and win over.
What seemed at first disinterested dialectics, indulged
in for truth's sake, or at least as « evaporations » of
wit, sounds quite differently when the reader realises this
dumb presence.

Of downright dialogue I find no instance in Donne,
unless it be the « ecclogue » which serves as a prelude
(and also a postlude) to the Sommerset epithalamium :
it is chiefly a device for heaping additional flattery upon
the bride and bridegroom, and a courtly apology for absence at the wedding. In his satires Donne sometimes
gives the words of his victims in the direct style, not
without liveliness. But in the *Songs and Sonets* we have
no such *carmen amœbæum* as, say, Horace's with Lydia :
Donec gratus eram tibi.... Donne's manner is at once

---

(32) Perhaps this is the sense adopted by Professor Grierson (volume
II of his edition, pp. XXXIV and XLII , but he does not explicitly distinguish it from the other senses ; he seems to use « passionate » and
« vivid » as equivalents to « dramatic » ; yet the comparisons between
Donne and Browning in the first passage, between Donne and Drayton
in the second, lead directly to a definition of the dramatic lyric. The
famous sonnet :

Since there's no help, come let us kiss and part...

is indeed the dramatic lyric *par excellence.* (See Emile Legouis, *Dans les
sentiers de la Renaissance anglaise. Les Belles-Lettres,* 1925, pp. 43-45). It
was published only in the 1619 edition of *Idea.*

more refined and more abrupt : it taxes the reader's imagination more severely ; it lacks the ease of the latin poet's dramatic lyric and has not such a wide appeal ; but it grows upon the imagination and repays minute study.

The four pieces which go by the common title of *Valediction* are dramas of the simplest kind. In one of them at least, possibly in others, the mistress from whom the poet-lover parts is weeping. But the interest centres on the symbol which provides three of the pieces with their subtitles : *of my name*, *in the window*, — *of the booke*, — *of weeping ;* — and though Donne called the fourth *A Valediction : forbiding mourning*, the reader will be sure to remember it as the piece in which the parted lovers are compared to « stiffe twin compasses ». — The song *Sweetest love, I do not goe* is to all intents and purposes a valediction, though Donne did not choose to entitle it so, perhaps because there was no symbol in it to emphasize its difference in sameness ; but it is all the more touching for the directness of its appeal, since attention is not withdrawn from the characters and the scene to a mere term of comparison. — *Breake of day* also is a valediction, more precisely a descendant of the medieval *aube* as Professor Grierson points out. Here, for once in the *Songs and Sonets*, the woman speaks, and so well that this piece alone would suffice to prove Donne's ability to express the feelings of others, and allow us to surmise that even when the speaker is a man he need not be the poet's own self. *Breake of day* stands not unworthy of comparison with the parting scene in *Romeo and Juliet*. True we hear in it no lark's song, which the lovers would persuade themselves to be the nightingale's ; no « jocund day

— Stands tiptoe on the misty mountain tops ». The language is as naked as can be, but its very nakedness speaks passion :

> 'Tis true, 'tis day ; what though it be?
> O wilt thou therefore rise from me?
> Why sould we rise, because 'tis light?
> Did we lie downe, because 'twas night?
> Love which in spight of darknesse brought us hether,
> Should in despight of light keepe us together.

This is the reading of the editions ; some of the manuscripts, Professor Grierson tells us, heighten the dialogue suggestion by punctuating line 3 thus :

> Why should we rise? Because 'tis light?

The first note of interrogation makes the symmetry with the next line less perfect, which may turn the scale in favour of the comma substituted for it by the editions : yet I cannot help preferring the more impassioned address, the short, panting questions, eagerly gasped out. The man's excuse, though unexpressed, is anticipated by the woman. Similarly in the last stanza he pleads, or is supposed to be ready to plead, the call of his professional duties :

> Must businesse thee from hence remove?

The woman's anger against that bloodless rival sounds natural and sincere in its exaggeration :

> On, that's the worst disease of love,
> The poore, the foule, the false, love can
> Admit, but not the busied man.

But the final couplet smacks of epigrammatic wit :

> He which hath businesse, and makes love, doth doe
> Such wrong. as when a maryed doth wooe.

The piece ends less dramatically than it began. But in

Shakespeare also, at least in the earlier plays, do not the characters often parade their (or rather the playwright's) ingenuity after crying out what their hearts feel ? The mixture is distinctly Elizabethan.

In *The Sunne Rising* we find the same situation and a similar feeling ; but here the lover addresses the sun, and his railings sound more rhetorical than dramatic. Yet the scenery, sketched in a few skilful strokes, redeems the piece from the fault of ranting in cold blood : the sunrays peer through windows and drawn curtains into the bed, a property only alluded to in *Breake of day* but here brazenly mentioned in the concluding lines of the last two stanzas, so as to leave us in no doubt of its paramount importance :

> Aske for those Kings whom thou saw'st yesterday,
> And thou shalt heare, All here in one bed lay.
>
> Shine here to us, and thou art every where ;
> This bed thy center is, these walls, thy spheare.

The good-morrow seems related to the foregoing group of poems, but the connexion is merely metaphorical. The lovers are not parting, neither does the sun remind them it were time to part. Their souls, not their bodies, have just awakened. Their happiness is for the nonce unalloyed; they wonder how they lived before they loved. Therefore the dramatic element appears less vividly than in those pieces where there is fear, or at least a sense that joy is ephemeral. Yet *The good-morrow* is no madrigal indited in the closet to a distant mistress ; it is the report of an impassioned dialogue in that « little room » where the lovers have met and which has become to them « an every where ». The woman remains silent, or rather her words are not given ; but her presence is felt : « *her* face in *his* eye, *his* in *hers* appeares ». — Let no one misunderstand me : this piece *was* written by Donne in his closet, and with much care ; it was revised by him (see Professor Grierson's note on the various readings of the manuscripts and editions) at leisure : what I mean is that it succeeds in creating a voluptuous atmosphere and calling up in it two flesh-and-blood human beings who act in relation to each other. The impression of passionate reality made upon the reader results partly from the poet's artfully concealed art, an art which is nothing if not dramatic.

However, against the applying of this epithet to *The good-morrow*, as indeed to almost every one of the pieces we have considered so far, it might be objected that they lack progression ; the situation and even the feelings are at the end what they were at the beginning. But there remain for study a few of the *Songs and Sonets* in which Donne's technique shows itself more complex : the initial situation evolves more or less, there are episodes and vicissitudes, or at least development.

The song « *Sweetest Love, I do not goe...* » differs, as we have noted, from the *Valedictions* in that it appeals to the heart, not through the medium of a symbol, but directly. It also gives more importance to the woman's part. The poet really speaks to her, not above her head, and he alters his tone according to the effect produced upon her by what he has just said. In the first stanza he tries to make her smile ; but we see that he fails, since the second stanza more seriously attempts to comfort her by promising a speedy return. Yet this also proves unavailing, and he, feeling helpless at the sight of her redoubling

grief, gives vent in the third stanza to his own despond-
ency. Man, he generalizes, « cannot add another houre »
to his good fortune, « nor a lost houre recall » ; but we
know how to assist misery when it comes and « teach it
art and length, — It selfe o'r us to'advance ». Such
sombre wisdom rather justifies the woman's grief as being
consonant to human nature. So in the fourth stanza he
returns to their own sad plight and entreats her to spare
him ; her grief is his death :

> When thou sigh'st, thou sigh'st not winde,
> But sigh'st my soule away,
> When thou weep'st, unkindly kinde,
> My lifes blood doth decay.

Besides, adds the first half of the fifth stanza, foreseeing
of evil will bring it to pass. Pity, with a touch of super-
stition in it, succeeds where wit, sense, philosophy, have
been of no avail. And now she listens, outwardly quieter,
to his renewed invitation to make light of his absence, and
to his assurance that no separation ever takes place between those « who one another keepe — Alive ». Thus
interpreted dramatically, this beautiful piece achieves a
unity which was not apparent when one considered it as
a lyric of the ordinary type. The reader must fill the logical gaps with kisses and embraces, sighs and sobs, weeping and the wiping away of tears, and gazings into the
woman's eyes to read her thoughts ; he must also realize
the failure of the lover's first efforts in order to understand the crescendo of pathos, and the relative success that
ensues so as to appreciate the more subdued and pacified
tone of the conclusion.

The Canonization stands alone among the *Songs and
Sonets* because the person addressed in it is a male friend,

but love is still the theme. The character who is speaking rejects the wordly-wise advice offered to him and vindicates his own abandonment to passion. The *motif* had been treated a few years before by Sir Philip Sidney in sonnet XIV of *Astrophel and Stella :*

> Alas, have I not paine enough my friend,
> ....
> But with your rubarbe wordes you must contend,
> To greeve me worse in saying, that desier
> Doth plunge my well form'd soule, even in the mier
> Of sinfull thoughtes, which doe in ruine end?

The sestet defiantly repudiates the charge :

> If that be sinne which doth the manners frame,
> Well stayed with trueth in worde and faith of deede,
> Readie of wit, and fearing nought but shame ;
> If that be sin which in fixt hartes doth breede,
> A loathing of all loose unchastitie ;
> Then love is sin, and let me sinfull bee.

Sidney resumes the debate in sonnet XXI :

> Your words my friend (right healthful causticks) blame
> My young minde marde whom Love doth windlase so :
> That my owne writings like bad servants shew
> My wits, quick in vaine thoughts, in vertue lame ;...

And after repeating the arguments of his well-meaning critics he concludes :

> Sure you say well, your wisedomes golden myne
> Dig deepe with learnings spade : now tell me this,
> Hath this world ought so faire as *Stella* is?

The difference between the two sonnets appears at once : in the former the poet glories in his love as an incitement to virtue ; in the latter he pleads guilty (33) and merely

---

(33) At least in the text of 1598 which I have adopted in the quotations. The first edition (1591) not unfrequently prints downright nonsense (as in l. 13 of sonnet XIV), but its reading in l. 1 of sonnet XXI is not impossible :

> Your words my freends me causelessly doe blame.

If Sidney wrote that, he no more pleaded guilty in this sonnet than in

excuses himself on the strength of the temptation (though
we may suspect his acknowledgement of « decline » from
youthful promise to be ironical). But either sonnet expresses one mood only, as it should do, while *The Canoniza-*
tion appears almost incoherent at the first reading, so
much does the tone (not the theme) change in the course
of its five stanzas. Of these the title fits only the last two ;
the first three have nothing to do with the admitting of the
lovers to the calendar of saints. To discover the essential
unity of the piece one must analyse it in a detailed
manner.

The famous opening line :

> For Godsake hold your tongue, and let me love,

shows us Donne at his best in the brusque familiar style.
In the rest of the stanza he makes fun of himself :

> Or chide my palsie, or my gout,
> My five gray haires, or ruin'd fortune flout,

and then of his friend :

> Observe his honour, or his grace,
> Or the Kings reall, or his stamped face
> Contemplate, what you will, approve,

but shows all the strength of his passion in the appeal : do
anything

> So you will let me love.

The satirical note reappears in the second stanza, where

---

the preceding one ; but without the initial admission the final tercet
loses much of its point :

> Well said, your wit in vertues golden myne
> Digs deepe...

(the rest as in the 1598 text quoted above). — Apart from that, the dramatic movement appears as clearly in the earlier edition, published
when Donne was eighteen, as in the later, published when he had
written most of his *Songs and Sonets*, if Ben Jonson is to be trusted.

it sounds still more clearly. The first line states the simple thought in simple terms :

> Alas, alas, who's injur'd by my love?

The next lines are a rhetorical amplification of that thought. The poet here parodies the hyperbolical metaphors of the Petrarchists, used elsewhere by himself more seriously :

> What merchants ships have my sighs drown'd?
> Who saies my teares have overflow'd his ground?
> When did my colds a forward spring remove?
> When did the heats which my veines fill
> Adde one more to the plaguie Bill?

In the last three lines satire becomes more stinging ; it still hits the love-poets who have exaggerated the influence of their heart-beats upon the world at large, but it also exposes the selfishness of the professional man :

> Soldiers finde warres, and Lawyers finde out still
> Litigious men, which quarrels move,
> Though she and I do love.

Among the accusations from which the lover pretends to be particularly anxious to clear himself, he places last, as the most heinous, that of having stopped all wars and law-suits, which would have brought upon him the just anger of two dangerous and vindictive kinds of men.

After this ironical outburst the lover pauses awhile to catch his breath, and the friend tries to get a word in. He upbraids the passionate couple with lack of sense : they are night-moths dazzled by a light. This speech, which takes place, if we may coin the word, in the inter-stanza, turns the lover's ardour from satire to self-glorification. So far he has told others to mind their own business and proved the harmlessness of his own all-engrossing pursuit; that strain recurs in the third stanza :

> Call her one, mee another flye,
> We'are Tapers too, and at our owne cost die,

which means : nobody suffers a loss by our death. But the
main idea now is that of justification by love :

> Call us what you will, wee are made such by love,

— nay, more, than justification, ennoblement :

> And wee in us finde the'Eagle and the Dove.

Probably the metaphor of the birds was suggested by
that of the insects, and corrects it ; in the erotic-mystical
language of the time « eagle » stands for « strength » and
« dove » for « tenderness and purity » ; let us remember
Crashaw's rapturous appeal to Saint Theresa :

> By all the eagle in thee, all the dove. (34)

But the metaphor of the Phenix, which comes up in the
next line and proceeds from that of the self-burning night-
moth, makes it likely that the eagle and the dove also arise
from fire. When Joan of Arc died, a dove was seen ascend-
ing to Heaven (the same miracle probably happened at
many another martyr's burning) ; and the Romans would
let fly an eagle from near the pyre of their emperors : Dry-
den, at that time very much a disciple of Donne, recalls
that rite in the first of his *Heroick Stanzas* on the death
of Oliver Cromwell (35). — Anyhow, with the Phenix
Donne openly reverts to the type of traditional hyperbole

---

(34) *The Flaming Heart, ad finem.*
(35)   And now 'tis time, for their officious haste,
                Who would before have borne him to the sky,
            Like eager Romans, ere all rites were past,
                Did let too soon the sacred eagle fly.
The stanzas were written after the funeral.

he has just ridiculed, but he wears the hackneyed symbol
with a difference :

> The Phœnix ridle hath more wit
> By us, we two being one, are it.

The fabulous bird, being unique of its kind, united in
himself both sexes ; the two lovers, having combined into
one « neutrall » (not a very happy substitute for « herm-
aphrodite ») thing, have also acquired that other property
of the phenix : they « dye and rise the same » as before.

Here the friend once more gets a chance and must be
understood prosaically to object that, unless the poet
means the metaphorical deaths and resurrections of parting and meeting again, he is straying very far from the
truth : their love may well destroy the lovers, but not call
them back to this nether world, not even provide them
with a living while they are in it. The fourth stanza admits the hard fact, but answers defiantly :

> Wee can dye by it, if not live by love.

It then proceeds to improve upon a hint given in the last
line of the third stanza : the love of the pair is a mystery ;
therefore they will have a «legend», *i. e.* their marvellous
but true story will be written for the edification of the
faithful in after ages ; their fame will rest safely, if not
in a « Chronicle », at least in « hymns ». This last word,
with its religious import, leads up naturally to the an-
nouncement that the poet and his mistress will be «*Canon-
iz'd* for love», on which the fourth stanza ends. The
friend this time probably opens his mouth to remonstrate
against pride amounting to blasphemy, if he is a Roman
catholic, or idolatry if he is a protestant ; but no word

of his can be even overheard, for the fourth stanza runs
into the fifth, without a period. The new-made saints are
already « invoked » by lovers who come after them ; their
intercession is prayed for in the most approved papistical
style ; the repetition of the words « You whom », « You to
whom...; who... » suggests a litany. Here Donne the lover
turns to good account the learning of Donne the schoolman, and, in the impassioned subtleties of that imaginary
address, the reader may well forget the friend who was
the occasion of the piece. Yet without him, and unless
we fill in his interruptions, we do not thoroughly realize
why the lover-poet gradually warms himself up and
passes from jesting impatience to an almost ecstatic
vision.

These last words naturally call to our minds the title
of another among the *Songs and Sonets*, which recent
critics generally agree in praising as the finest and most
characteristic of all, but of which they give divergent
interpretations, none of then, I think, adequate. *The
Extasie* resembles *The Canonization* in its use of scholastic
notions for lyric-dramatic effect ; it differs from the piece
we have just analysed because it is partly narrative and
the dumb character, here a woman, takes no such active
share in the dramatic part as the male friend did. On the
other hand the scenery is described in *The Extasie* at
greater length than in any other of Donne's lyrics (except
The Primrose, which is not dramatic), but the description
assumes, so to speak, the form of a stage-direction, instead
of occuring in the speeches themselves, after the more
artistic manner of *The Apparition* and *The Sunne Rising* :

Where, like a pillow on a bed,
A Pregnant banke swel'd up, to rest

> The violets reclining head,
> Sat we two, one anothers best.

Donne is no poet of nature ; his proper study is man ;
even when he for once lays the scene of his action out-
doors, his metaphors take us back to the boudoir or the
rake's den. The epithet « pregnant », though not voluptuous, is also sexual, and the drooping violets suggest
languor. The feelings of the lovers are in keeping with
the place ; indeed, rather than feelings I should say sen-
sations :

> Our hands were firmely cimented
> With a fast balme, which thence did spring.

In like words but with bitter irony Othello praises Des-
demona's hand, « moist..., hot, hot, and moist », which
« argues fruitfulness and liberal heart », but warns her
against the « young and sweating devil » there. — Donne
goes on :

> Our eyes-beames twisted, and did thred
> Our eyes, upon one double string.

Generally sight, of all the senses, expresses love most
spiritually ; but here looking into each other's eyes
becomes as material a link as joining hands. The metaphor of the string threading the two balls would reach
the acme of bad taste if it did not fitly convey the physical
intensity of the situation. — The next stanza, ostensibly
telling us what has not yet taken place between the
lovers, hints it were time it took place, and so puts the
problem which is the *raison d'être* of the whole piece :

> So to'entergraft our hands, as yet
> Was all the meanes to make us one,
> And pictures in our eyes to get
> Was all our propagation.

But the poet would defeat his own purpose if he opened it too clearly and too soon. He has said enough of the bodies for the nonce, and now passes to the souls whose meeting he depicts in the loftiest language ; he insists upon the perfect stillness of the lovers in order to emphasize their Platonic purity :

> As 'twixt two equall Armies, Fate
> Suspends uncertaine victorie,
> Our soules, (which to advance their state,
> Were gone out, hung 'twixt her, and mee.
> And whil'st our soules negociate there,
> Wee like sepulchrall statues lay ;
> All day, the same our postures were,
> And wee said nothing, all the day.

Even words are too gross, it seems, for such ethereal passion ; but the cynical reader remembers the balm cementing the hands, and smiles. Donne, however, preserves a most serious countenance, and introduces an hypothetical listener who bears witness to the ennobling quality of the scene :

> If any, so by love refin'd,
> That he soules language understood,
> And by good love were growen all minde,
> Within convenient distance stood,
> He (though, he knew not which soule spake,
> Because both meant, both spake the same)
> Might thence a new concoction take,
> And part farre purer then he came.

So ends the narrative prelude to the speech which contains the gist of the matter. Let us note the use of the preterite to report the circumstances in which the incident happened. It is undramatic ; so is the introduction of a third party whom the poet does not even invest with more than a virtual existence. And the reader is puzzled, because the poet has not frankly taken him into his confidence though he has thrown out hints of an unscrupulous and selfish scheme veiled behind transcendental pretence.

As soon as the speech begins, one thing at least becomes clear : the supposed impossibility for the listener to tell whose voice he heard and the ensuing use of « we » instead of « I » are mere flattery and wile on the lover's part. The woman will feel pleased, her vanity will be tickled when she thinks she is considered able to utter such high-flown conceits ; she will not notice the moment when it is no longer safe for her to agree to the man's metaphysics, which she interprets with a weaker head and more fervid heart.

The first half of the speech (ll. 29-48) exalts Platonic love and explains its workings :

> This Extasie doth unperplex
> (We said) and tell us what we love,
> Wee see by this, it was not sexe,
> Wee see, we saw not what did move :

As Professor Grierson points out, that theory of the new insight acquired in ecstasy comes, directly or indirectly, from Plotinus ; and so does that of the contact and union of souls in the next lines :

> But as all severall soules containe
> Mixture of things, they know not what,
> Love, these mixt soules, doth mixe againe,
> And makes both one, each this and that.

The poet, however, stops borrowing to insert one of his curiously matter-of-fact comparisons, at once familiar and unexpected :

> A single violet transplant,
> The strength, the colour, and the size,
> (All which before was poore, and scant,)
> Redoubles still, and multiplies.

After « transplant » the reader must supply : « to a richer soil » ; the remark sounds like a sensible gardener's, not an idle dilettante's (36). Indeed it does not interrupt the logical process, being neither emotional nor picturesque , the poet is reasoning by anology, as Bacon himself so often does : a violet improves by transplanting, so will a soul :

> When love, with one another so
> Interinanimates two soules,
> That abler soule, which thence doth flow,
> Defects of loneliness controules.
> Wee then, who are this new soule, know,
> Of what we are compos'd and made,...

These last two lines take us back to the new insight, for which the preceding ones have sufficiently accounted ; they are the logical conclusion of that half of the speech : the demonstration of the superior quality of Platonic love seems now complete. But the poet goes on with it, and rather impairs it from the philosopher's point of view :

> For, th'Atomies of which we grow,
> Are soules, whom no change can invade.

Grammar will hardly admit of any other antecedent to « whom » than « soules ». If so, one might well ask how

---

(36) Gosse, II, 75-6, who speaks of *The Extasie* as an « extremely fantastic lyric », owns himself puzzled by « its obsession on the word « violet » ; this had, unquestionably, at the time of its composition an illuminating meaning which time has completely obscured ». But the difficulty grows much less if we call upon Donne to provide his own commentary ; in his funeral sermon on Magdalen Herbert, Lady Danvers ; he says (Logan Pearsall Smith, *op. cit.*, p. 39) : « But in that *ground*, her Fathers family, shee grew not many yeeres. Transplanted young from thence, by mariage, into another *family* of *Honour*, as a flower that doubles and multiplies by transplantation, she multiplied into *ten Children...* » — Gosse diffidently classes *The Extasie* among the poems written by Donne « between his great criminal liaison and his ultimate betrothal », and ascribes it « to the same vague category of emotions which faintly stirred the poet » in that interval as *The Blossome*.

the « mixture of things » scornfully mentioned in l. 34, has now become an « atomy », something perfectly simple and pure. But Donne may well risk this sophism ; he knows the woman has been out of her intellectual depth for some time, and wants anyhow to impress her with the notion that they are now secure from change, whatever they do.

Now the lover boldly comes to the point and says what he has been thinking of all the time :

> But O alas, so long, so farre
> Our bodies why doe wee forbeare ?

And without allowing the woman time to consider this startling proposition by the light of her own moral sense, he hastens to ply her with arguments for consenting. He appeals now to her reason, somewhat stunned by this time :

> They are ours, though they are not wee, wee are
> The intelligences, they the spheare,

(remember that in line 20 the bodies were « wee »), now to her feeling, namely gratitude :

> We owe them thankes, because they thus,
> Did us, to us, at first convay,
> Yeelded their forces, sense, to us,
> Nor are drosse to us, but allay.

But reason is better ; the woman will mistrust it less readily, and the compliment paid to her as one above her sex in intellect will go a long way towards removing her last scruples ; besides, the lover's reputation as a casuist requires that he should at least seem to reconcile the two sharply opposed definitions of love that he has just been and is now giving. Scientific comparisons will be helpful, first an astrological one :

> On man heavens influence workes not so,
>> But that it first imprints the ayre,
> Soe soule into the soule may flow,
>> Through it to body first repaire ;

secondly a physiological one :

> As our blood labours to beget
>> Spirits, as like soules as it can,
> Because such fingers need to knit
>> That subtile knot, which makes us man :
> So must pure lovers soules descend
>> T'affections, and to faculties,
> Which sense may reach and apprehend, (36 *bis*)
>> Else a great Prince in prison lies.

In the last line the appeal to reason again passes into an appeal to feeling, no longer gratitude but pity, that most insidious enemy to virtue in woman as in man. The magnificent language takes us very far above the seducer's scheme, and alone explains Coleridge's selection of *The Extasie* for special praise : « I should never find fault with metaphysical poems if they were all like this or but half as excellent ». But immediately after this flight we fall back to earth :

> To'our bodies turne wee then, that so
>> Weake men on love reveal'd may looke ;
> Loves mysteries in soules doe grow,
>> But yet the body is his booke.
> And if some lover, such as wee,
>> Have heard this dialogue of one,
> Let him still marke us, he shall see
>> Small change, when we'are to bodies gone.

(36 *bis*) In his frankly sensual poem, *A rapture*, Carew uses some-what similar language to set forth the reverse explanation :

> There a bed
> Of roses and fresh myrtles shall be spread,
> ... ...
> Whereon our panting limbs we'll gently lay,
> In the faint respites of our active play :
> That so our slumbers may in dreams have leisure
> To tell the nimble fancy our past pleasure,
> And so our souls, that cannot be embraced,
> Shall the embraces of our bodies taste.

Probably Coleridge read a spiritual meaning into these last two stanzas ; we may regret he did not write it down for us, since the plain and literal meaning sounds queer and unpleasant enough. The hypothetical listener of the prelude reappears and turns spectator at a time when the lovers as well as we could well wish him away. And is the woman so dazed that she should fail to suspect triumphant cynicism in that conclusion? Logical symmetry, however, receives this satisfaction that the final line of the second part of the speech repeats, with some variation, the last line of the first part : « no change » becomes « small change », the difference between the two terms representing what the man has won and the woman lost.

Donne, his latest biographer affirms, maintained his search for truth with a persistent honesty of purpose (37). If by truth is meant *adequatio spiritus et rei*, as the poet himself would have said, or objective truth, as the new schoolmen now say, I feel bound to disagree. Such truth in *The Extasie* at best occupies a very subordinate position. Donne does not set to solve once for all the difficult problem of the relations between soul and body in love (38). He considers the particular case of a couple who

---

(37) Payne, *op. cit.*, p. 19. — Rupert Brooke, in his review of Grierson's edition (*The Nation*, London, 15. II. 1913) already says : « Indeed Donne... heralded and in some part led this age when English literature climbed and balanced briefly on the difficult pinnacle of sincerity... One can never doubt his sincerity ». It is not easy, however, to ascertain what Rupert Brooke means by this word « sincerity ». He on the other hand repeatedly compares Donne to the contemporary English dramatists without exactly saying that Donne's art is dramatic, much less how it is dramatic. And to him Marston's dramas, Jonson's additions to the *Spanish tragedy*, Shakespeare's *Hamlet* and *Measure for Measure*, Webster's plays, are sincere and tragic in the same sense as Donne's lyrics.

(38) With all due deference to Professor Grierson, I submit that he has taken *The Extasie* too seriously. It is serious in this sense that the man passionately desires the woman, but not as an attempt « to transcend...

have been playing at Platonic love, sincerely enough on the woman's part, and imagines how they would pass from it to carnal enjoyment ; whether he thinks this *in abstracto* a natural consummation or a sad falling off matters little ; the chief interest of the piece is psychological, and character being represented here in action, dramatic. The heroine remains indeed for the reader to shape, but the hero stands before us, self-revealed in his hypocritical game. If truth exists here, it is the truth that we find in the speeches of Molière's Don Juan, who can call on Heaven when convenient and cloak his wicked designs in religious cant, the truth of the playwright who holds up the mirror to human nature (39).

---

the dualism... » which was the conventional theory of man's nature in Donne's time (*ut supra*, vol. II, pp. XLVI-XLVII). I am ready to admit that if Donne had stated his disinterested views on the subject they would have been very much those which Professor Grierson describes ; I only question his having done so in *The Extasie*. — Massingham p. 335, seems to hold the same opinion of Donne's sincerity in this piece.

(39) Don Juan's hypocrisy, it is well known, connects him with Tartuffe whose addresses to Elmire should also be compared with *The Extasie*. In all these characters the influence of the worse sort of Spanish Jesuits appears very clearly. — It is a far cry from Donne to Pailleron, but I see a close parallel to *The Extasie* in *Le monde où l'on s'ennuie*, Act III, scene IV, where Bellac (a caricature of the spiritualistic philosopher Caro) wooes one of Donne's fellow-countrywomen. Lucy, more argumentative than the heroine of *The Extasie*, denies the existence of Platonic love.

BELLAC : Voyons, Lucy, un exemple. Supposons deux êtres quelconques — deux abstractions — deux entités — un homme quelconque — une femme quelconque, tous deux s'aiment, mais de l'amour .vulgaire, physiologique, vous me comprenez ?
LUCY : Parfaitement !
BELLAC : Je les suppose dans une situation comme celle-ci, seuls la nuit, ensemble, que va-t-il arriver ?... Fatalement ! — suivez-moi bien ; — fatalement, il va se produire le phénomène que voici... Tous deux, ou plus vraisemblablement, l'un des deux, le premier, l'homme... se rapprochera de celle qu'il croit aimer... (Il s'approche d'elle).
LUCY (se reculant un peu) : Mais...
BELLAC (la retenant doucement) : Non, non !.. Vous allez voir ! Ils plongeront leurs regards dans leurs regards ; ils mêleront leurs souffles et leurs chevelures...
LUCY : Mais, Monsieur Bellac...
BELLAC : Et alors !... Et alors !... il se passera en leur moi... indépendamment de leur moi lui-même, une suite non interrompue d'actes inconscients, qui, par une sorte de progrès, de processus lent, mais inéluc-

In the scholastic Don Juan of *The Extasie*, has Donne
portrayed himself ? Is this piece the record of one youthful adventure of his ? The answer to this question, even
if it were safe to answer it, lies beyond the scope of this
essay (40). At any rate the supposition contains no internal improbability, since Donne was sensual, yet dabbled in
platonics ; he certainly resembled his hero closely, while
Molière had very little of the Spanish libertine, least of
all his hypocrisy. This amounts to saying that Donne's

---

table, les jettera, si j'ose dire, à la fatalité d'un dénouement prévu ou
la volonté ne sera pour rien, l'intelligence pour rien, l'âme pour rien !
LUCY : Permettez !... ce processus...
BELLAC : Attendez, attendez !... Supposons maintenant un autre cou-
ple et un autre amour ; à la place de l'amour physiologique, l'amour psy-
chologique ; à la place d'un couple quelconque, — deux exceptions...
vous me suivez toujours ?
LUCY : Oui.
BELLAC : Eux aussi, assis l'un près de l'autre, se rapprocheront l'un
de l'autre.
LUCY (s'éloignant encore) : Mais alors c'est la même chose !
BELLAC (la retenant toujours) : Attendez donc ! Il y a une nuance.
Laissez-moi vous faire voir la nuance. Eux aussi pourront plonger leurs
yeux dans leurs yeux et mêler leurs chevelures...
LUCY : Mais enfin ? (Elle se lève).
BELLAC (la faisant rasseoir) : Seulement !... Seulement !... Ce n'est plus
leur beauté qu'ils contemplent, c'est leur âme ; ce n'est plus leur voix
qu'ils entendent, c'est la palpitation même de leur pensée ! Et lorsque
enfin, par un processus tout autre, quoique congénère, ils en seront ar-
rivés, eux aussi, à ce point obscur et troublé où l'être s'ignore lui-même,
sorte d'engourdissement délicieux du vouloir qui paraît être à la fois
le *summum* et le *terminus* des félicités humaines, ils ne se réveilleront pas
sur la terre, eux, mais en plein ciel, car leur amour à eux plane bien
par delà les nuages orageux des passions communes dans le pur éther
des idéalités sublimes !
Lucy is « troublée », then « tout à fait émue », though she keeps
objecting with less and less energy. The scene would probably end like
The Extasie, if the characters who have been listening to the dialogue
were of the same cast as Donne's admiring spectator. — Of course
Pailleron's Voltairian irony is less subtle and complex than Donne's,
more conscious too of its own aim, but the chief difference between the
two scenes lies in the prose of the one and the verse of the other.

(40) Payne, pp. 94-5, indeed makes Anne More the heroine of *The
Extasie* and calls this « a poem which shows that Donne had attained to
a realization of the nature of true love... ; he has... solved the problem
of the place in life of sex ». The mere choice of a bank of violets for
the scene of this incident, not to mention the presence of a spectator,
even one « by love refined », and the coarseness of the conclusion, ren-
ders it both unlikely and undesirable that married love should be the
theme of *The Extasie*. Yet one must own that Payne's supposition provides the best, and perhaps the only, way of clearing the hero from
the charge of hypocrisy, by making him a considerate bridegroom.

dramatic power mostly worked upon his personal experience, however freely he may have dealt with the setting and circumstances of each incident. *The Extasie* is the strongest of the *Songs and Sonets*, not because it reveals his final creed about love, but because it pictures the type of lover he knew most intimately, from the inside, and no other poet ever knew and sympathized with so well as he.

Leaving Donne the man, let us return to Donne the poet : Signor Mario Praz has excellently shown that the scholastic propositions in his verse are but a barrister's special pleadings ; medieval philosophy he regards not as a complete explanation of the universe but as « an arsenal » of arguments ; his reason for choosing some and neglecting others is « practical rather than speculative ». The Italian critic adds : « And the practical reason of Donne is an intellectual diversion », which consists in « the exercise of wit » ; in other words the poet aims at using and showing his dialectical skill (41). This last statement requires correction : in not a few of the *Songs and Sonets* the barrister pleads, disingenuously indeed, but earnestly enough, because he pleads for himself, not before an

---

(41) *Secentismo...* p. 100 : « La base culturale del Donne è certamente medievale, ma in quella multifaria scienza egli sceglie come in un arsenale i suoi argomenti ; non coordinandoli a un sistema, a un pensiero centrale, ma servendosene come di espedienti curialeschi, in vista della loro acconcezza al caso singolo : non convincimenti metafisci si tratta, ma di divertimenti metafisici. C'è insomma tra un poeta medievale e il Donne una differenza simile a quella che intercede tra un giurista e un avoccato : il primo sviluppa da certe premesse fondamentali tutto un sistema di coordinazioni e di corollari, il secondo cerca dovechessia gli argomenti che tornano in favore del suo caso, non perchè si senta più persuaso della loro verità che di quella dei loro contrari, ma per una ragione pratica anzichè speculativa. E la ragione pratica del Donne è il divertimento dell'intelligenza : il gusto che egli prova nella sua indagine è non già quello della ricerca della verità (come presso i medievali), sibbene quello dell'esercizio dell' ingegno ». Cf. also, pp. 103-6, the analysis of *The Extasie* by Praz, who insists upon the difference between Donne's scholasticism and Dante's.

academic jury of literary connoisseurs, but with the one woman whom he loves for the nonce. Persuading her to yield is the practical reason which decides upon the lover's choice of arguments and manner of presenting them. Seen in this light, even such a symmetrical piece of work as *The Prohibition* reveals a dramatic aspect which had so far escaped us. We took it for granted that the lover twice changed his mind : between the first and the second stanzas, then between the second and the third ; if we read the piece again we begin to suspect that, here as in *The Extasie*, he knew from the start where he wanted to go , he tacked twice in the road the more surely to enter the haven of his mistress's love when he put about the third time. We disbelieve the abnegation with which he pretends to regard only his mistress's interest, not his own. And in the final line :

To let mee live, O love and hate mee too,

we surmise that the admixture of hate is intended only to salve the woman's conscience. The tone differs much, but the object little, from those of *The Dampe*, where the lover tells her who kills him with the help of « th'enormous Gyant, *her* Disdaine », and « th'enchantresse Honor » :

Kill mee as Woman, let mee die
As a meere man ; doe you but try
Your passive valor, and you shall finde than,
In that you'have odds enough of any man.

And one finds the same suit again in the two pieces which exhibit Donne's dramatic art in its most complex form, and which therefore I have kept for the end of this study, *The Flea* and *The Dreame*.

Extravagantly admired in the XVII [th] century, not only by the erratic English but by the staid Dutch, *The*

Flea has been pilloried again and again since good taste
set in, as Donne's worst offence against literary, if not
against moral, propriety. But it seems that both those
who praised and those who censured the piece thought
only of the hyperbolical conceits : in the second stanza
the mingling of the lovers' blood in the flea's belly is said
to be almost a marriage, yea more than that ; the insect
becomes at once woman, man, nuptial bed, and wedding
church ; in killing it the poet's mistress would commit,
not only murder on him, a crime she is inured to, but sui-
cide and sacrilege. Yet there is cleverness of another, and
less obsolete, kind in *The Flea* ; the scene it describes
has the liveliness of the animal which plays there such a
prominent part. So far Donne has given us scenes with
two characters in them ; here we have a third, much
more real and active than the imaginary spectator in *The
Extasie*. And while a painter might represent *The Apparition* all on one canvas, it would take a suite of three
pictures to reproduce the attitudes in *The Flea*. Number
one, the man is pointing to the insect which jumped from
him on to her :

> Marke but this flea, ...
> It suck'd me first, and now sucks thee.

Number two, the woman is hunting the flea, perhaps
she has already caught it, and the man tries to dissuade
her from putting it to death :

> Oh stay, three lives in one flea spare.

Number three, the woman has disregarded the man's
petition and crushed the once « living walls of Jet » ; a
vivid contrast of colours ensues :

> Cruell and sodaine, hast thou since
> Purpled thy naile, in blood of innocence?

Whatever pity he may feel for the victim, the man does
not forget his own plea. Indeed the woman seems to have
killed the insect less out of revenge than to vindicate the
moral law questioned by the man on the strength of the
insect's practice. He had told her :

> .... marke in this,
> How little that which thou deny'st me is ;
> ....
> And in this flea, our two bloods mingled bee ;
> Thou know'st that this cannot be said
> A sinne, nor shame, nor losse of maidenhead,
>   Yet this enjoyes before it wooe,
>   And pamper'd swells with one blood made of two,
>   And this, alas, is more then wee would doe.

By punishing the brute offender against her chastity the
woman has answered the man's sophism ; but the latter
does not accept his defeat and undertakes to clear the
memory of the insect he has failed to save :

> Wherein could this flea guilty bee,
> Except in that drop which it suckt from thee?
> Yet thou triumph'st, and saist that thou
> Find'st not thy selfe, nor mee the weaker now ;

the conclusion is so obvious that the logician scorns to
complete his syllogism ; from the flea's innocency, so
well established, he passes at once to the harmlessness
of his own design upon the woman :

> 'Tis true, then learne how false, feares be ;
> Just so much honor, when thou yeeld'st to mee,
> Will wast, as this flea's death tooke life from thee.

This conclusion closely resembles that of *The Extasie*,
» just so much honor » in the one corresponding to « small
change » in the other. From the standpoint of drama-

tic craftsmanship, exception might be taken to the reporting of the woman's boast in the indirect style ; that is undoubtedly a little awkward, and, if the rule of the game forbids our hearing her, we would rather guess her retort than be told of it so bluntly. But apart from this fault, a small one in material extent, *The Flea* is good comedy, or, if one demurs to that word, good farce; its humour may appear rather low to the fastidious modern mind, but it did not transgress the rules of good breeding under Queen Elizabeth, of maiden fame.

Not less skilful in its technique, *The Dreame* expresses, if not purer, at least more poetical feelings. The scene is a room which we guess to be but dimly lit ; the man is lying, if not in bed, at least, it seems, on a couch. The woman comes in while he is dreaming of her, and sits by him. Her entrance wakes him and he thanks her for doing so : the dream was happy, but its theme suited reason, the capacity of a waking soul, better than fantasy, that of a sleeping soul (42). Yet, he goes on, this visit does not interrupt his dream, but continues it ; and he seizes upon the opportunity to pay a highly metaphysical compliment to his mistress : in God being and intelligence are one ; similarly

---

(42)   It was a theame
     For reason, much too strong for phantasie.

Cf. *Elegy* X, ll. 9-10 :

     When you are gone, and *Reason* gone with you,
     Then *Fantasie* is Queene and Soule, and all.

The elegy, which had not title in the 1633 edition, received that of *The Dreame* in the 1635 edition, wrongly, Professor Grierson suggests. Yet the similarities between it and the piece in the *Songs and Sonets* which bears the same title are curious ; the elegy also might be interpreted dramatically.

LIBRARY
OF
MOUNT ST. MARY'S
COLLEGE
EMMITSBURG, MARYLAND

> Thou art so truth, that thoughts of thee suffice,
> To make dreames truths ; and fables histories ; (43)

but the sensuous lover reappears at once, and we feel the
kind of truth he prizes so much might be called more
clearly by the name of reality :

> Enter these armes, for since thou thoughtst it best,
> Not to dreame all my dreame, let's act the rest.

The first stanza ends on this gesture of the man, one of
gentle entreaty, arms held out, a fond smile on the lips
and in the eyes.

The woman, it seems, remains seated, and out of
reach. So the man tries to lure her forward ; if he is not
Donne himself, at least he resembles him like a twin
brother in his use of scholastic theology. Here occurs the
already-mentioned apology to the woman for thinking her
at first sight to be an angel, and no more. But now we
realize that the hyperbolical wit does not aim at pleasing
any circle of fine gentlemen and ladies, except indirectly,
as part of a dramatic action : while we read the second
stanza we keep on seeing the stretched arms, and the
couch ; and the metaphysical subtleties reveal themselves
as amorous blandishments.

Now comes the peripeteia : the woman rises, not to
draw nearer but to go away. Is she afraid of her own
boldness ? Does she feel remorse already for jeopardizing
her virtue ? the lover asks himself ; more likely she is a
coquette and likes to play with fire. Perhaps, we may
add, she thinks the man rather tame, and laughs in her
sleeve at his too intellectual method of seduction :

---

(43) See in Grierson's note the quotation from Aquinas. One also
remembers in this connexion Saint Anselm's ontological proof of God's
existence.

Comming and staying show'd thee, thee,
But rising makes me doubt, that now,
   Thou art not thou.
That love is weake, where feare's as strong as hee ;
'Tis not all spirit, pure, and brave,
If mixture it of *Feare, Shame, Honor,* have.
Perchance as torches, which must ready bee,
Men light and put out, so thou deal'st with mee,
Thou cam'st to kindle, goest to come ; Then I
Will dreame that hope againe, but else would die.

The invective againts honour recalls that in *The Dampe*, but the tone is far more subdued. The lover's morality has not improved, but the dreamy atmosphere pervades his speech ; his fierceness has left him, at least temporarily ; even woman's manœuvre fails to rouse him. Yet, whatever estimate she may form of his softness, we see in it the proof of his genuine attachment, voluptuous indeed and not respectful, but tender and which harmonizes well with the setting of the scene. In *The Dreame* Donne's dramatic art achieves its most delicate success.

Browning's admiration for his metaphysical predecessor has often been noticed and commented upon. Yet no English critic, to my knowledge, has ever pointed out exactly this resemblance between them, due either to identity of temperament or conscious imitation on Browning's part. Professor Grierson indeed puts into the same class of poetry *The Last Ride together* or *Too late* and *The Extasie ;* but he adds to this *The Anniversarie*, which is not at all dramatic, though very passionate, and he defines each of these pieces « a record of intense, rapid thinking, expressed in the simplest, most appropriate language », contrasting them with a poem like *Come into the garden, Maud* by which thought is suspended and the mind filled « with a succession of picturesque and volup-

tuous images in harmony with the dominant mood » (44).
However true in itself, the remark seems to miss the
chief point that *The Extasie* and *The Last Ride together*,
for instance, have in common : their being impassioned
addresses spoken to interlocutors whose reactions we may
guess. *Too late* is more of a soliloquy pure and simple,
the lover addressing only the memory of his beloved. But
My last duchess, not mentioned by Professor Grierson,
seems to me as good an instance as any of Browning's
likeness and unlikeness to Donne. Let us compare it with
The Canonization : in both pieces we find a man telling
his love-story to another man whose questions or answers
we are not allowed to know directly, but whose sup-
pressed words, or gestures, or looks, we cannot leave out
of account without misunderstanding the movement of
the scene entirely. On the other hand we see no touch in
The Canonization of the local colour that is so conspicuous
in *My last duchess* : Donne's lover might be himself, or
one of his contemporaries ; the Italian despot of the Renaissance, sombre, jealous, and cruel, has nothing in common with the Mr. Browning who proved such a good
husband to Miss Elizabeth Barrett. The older poet is modern, the later poet is historical. Or, if one objects that
most of the Victorian's *dramatis personae* stand for per-
manent human types and that we must look through
their temporary trappings, let us say he makes the Elizabethan's dramatic lyric more dramatic and less lyrical (I
here take this last word in its meaning of « personal : that

---

(44) Vol. II, p. XXXIII. — Cf. *supra*, note 32.

expresses the author's own thoughts and feelings »). (45).
The artistic imagination which could create some
fifty *Men and women* in one còllection of verse certainly
played a small part as yet in the *Songs and Sonets*, where
it seldom, if ever, appeared unmixed with sentimental or
intellectual self-expression. Nevertheless the technique
Donne used to such effect remained substantially un-
altered when it was resumed, after a lapse of over two
centuries, by Browning : the latter's going out of himself
only enabled him to apply it more variously (46).

*
* *

It is for the reader to judge whether I have proved my
thesis. I only beg he will discount occasional overstate-
ments indulged in for clearness' sake, and also the general
one-sidedness which is inherent in an essay of this sort
but so often results in the exaggeration of a minor truth
to the detriment of greater truths. We have been looking,
so to speak, at Donne's hand through a magnifying-glass,
while his head and breast either remained outside our
field of vision or barely retained their normal size. In
a full-lengh portrait the proportions should of course be
restored, but I do not attempt this piece of work. I shall

---

(45) One remembers that Browning's comment upon Wordsworth's famous definition of Shakespeare's sonnets as the key with which the
dramatist opened his heart : « If so the less Shakespeare he ! », called
forth Swinburne's retort : « No whit the less like Shakespeare, but undoubtedly the less like Browning ».

(46) Among the poets of to-day Paul Géraldy has used the dramatic
lyric with great alertness in his verse-story, *Toi et moi* (Paris, Stock,
1913). The short pieces of which it is composed are linked together as
the *Songs and Sonets* are not, but each piece may be read as a whole
and compared to individual lyrics of Donne's. In both poets we find the
same emotional intensity (which, unlike Browning's, is or seems to be
the result of personal experience) and clever dramatic suggestion. —
The *Finale* of *Toi et moi* treats in a very modern and disillusioned way
the theme of Drayton's sixty-first sonnet.

merely sum up here the corrections suggested in these pages to the best existing criticisms of the poet.

Donne cared for art, or, to put it more unexceptionably, he was interested in technique. His life, at least his youth during which he wrote most of the *Songs and Sonets*, was wild, whether we consider the lover or the thinker in him ; but when he set to indite a love-poem, or vent in verse a theory on problems of sexual morality, he composed himself and looked about for literary devices to improve his theme ; or, if the first stanza of a piece shaped itself while his blood was still hot, he had to cool down before he proceeded to copy its metrical design accurately in the second and next stanzas. What has misled some critics is that he did not use the ordinary means of turning thought or feeling into poetry. He preferred new processes to safe ones, and not seldom paid the penalty of his venturesomeness. This shows most clearly in his versification, but it appears no less true when one studies the presentment of his lyrics.

It follows that biographers should fight shy of interpreting the *Songs and Sonets* as a record of Donne's love-affairs, except in the most general terms. Sir Edmund Gosse now and then laid himself open to the charge of recklessness, but we admire his restraint when we compare his great work to a recent romance, purporting to be a life of Donne. Professor Grierson very wisely warned us against the literalism that sees « an actual particular experience behind every sincere poem ». History, he went on, « refutes the idea of such a simple relation between experience and art. No poet will sing of love convincingly who has never loved, but that experience will suffice

him for many and diverse webs of song and drama » (47).
Yet he too fell, it seems to me, a victim to the biographical temptation when he suggested that this or that lyric
is addressed to Anne More, or Lady Bedford, or Mrs. Herbert. I have already noted that in the pieces which have
a dramatic setting strict indentification of the woman
and even of the man goes against artistic probability. I
shall only add that my scepticism extends to the non-
dramatic pieces. For instance I cannot believe that the
« sequence » including *The Funerall*, *The Blossome*, *The
Primrose*, *The Relique*, and *The Dampe*, was addressed
to Mrs Herbert, according to the conjecture that Professor Grierson repeatedly advances, sometimes with more
and sometimes with less caution (48).

More deep-reaching is the suspicion this study casts
upon the *Songs and Sonets* considered as fragments of a
metaphysical creed or system. Indeed critics have long
pointed out contradictions between the several pieces, and
divided these into two, or better three, groups differing
in tone and tendency. Of the first group, which includes
cynical professions of fickleness like *The Indifferent*,
Love Usury, *Confined Love*, it need hardly be demonstra-
ted that one should not build up a theory of free love
upon them, even though they borrow from theories then
in favour, as I have mentioned with reference to *Communitie*. Of the second group, which includes more or less
consistently Petrarchian or Platonic efforts like *The Funerall*, *The Primrose*, *The Relique*, *Twicknam garden*,
and *A nocturnall upon S. Lucies day*, Professor Grierson

<hr/>

(47) Vol. II, p. XXIII.
(48) See *infra*, appendix B.

admits that they are largely conventional and artificial.
Donne's originality revealing itself chiefly in an under-
tone of satire, or an amorous warmth hardly compatible
with the theories of love he is supposed to accept. But
in the third group, the poet, it is said, finds a middle way
between impertinent lust and frigid idealism ; there he
is most himself, and there we must look for his « philosophy » of complete love, « the meaning and end of which
is marriage » (49). Unfortunately this theory rests mostly
on *The Extasie*, and if one adopts my interpretation of the
piece it is in danger of falling to the ground. Signor Praz
has already reduced the importance of ideas in Donne's
poetry to juster proportions. This essay tries to show that
what earnestness there is in *The Songs and Sonets* often
belongs, not to the poet himself, but to the character he
presents, and the situation in which he places this
character.

Some, who have loved Donne for the intellectual quality of his poetry, may complain that I bring him down
to a lower sphere than that of pure enthusiasm for theor-
etical truth, and so degrade him. Of course the aim of such
a study as this is neither to degrade nor to exalt, but to
explain what can be explained in the mystery of poetical
composition. Moreover, what it deducts from qualities
which, high as they are, belong rather to the philosopher
than to the poet, it compensates for by recognizing in
Donne qualities that are more strictly artistic. He appears
more skilful, and more conscious of his skill. The craftsman in him goes halves with the thinker. And it may be

(49) Vol. II, p. XLV.

contended that Donne comes out of this examination, though not a greater, yet a still more complex and therefore a more interesting, personality.

APPENDIX A

The best explanation of the irregularities noted in Donne's verse, especially in his decasyllabics, is that given as early as *c.* 1760 by Gray in his *Observations on English metre*. Having said of the *Ægloga octava* of *The Shepheardes Calender* that in the beginning of it Spenser has given « an instance of the decasyllabic with an unusual liberty in the feet », Gray adds this footnote : « And after him Dr. Donne (in his *Satires*) observes no regularity in the pause, or in the feet of his verse, only the number of syllables is equal throughout. I suppose he thought this rough uncouth measure suited the plain familiar style of satirical poetry (1) ». The last remark has become a commonplace of later criticism, but the connexion between Spenser's *August* and Donne's *Satires* as regards scansion has been too often lost sight of, and various attempts, all doomed to failure, have been made to discover five feet in lines which Donne, if he thought of feet at all, intended to fall into four.

Let us take the first satire, containing 112 lines. Only one (l. 13) has less than ten syllables in the 1633 edition :

> First sweare by thy best love in earnest

and it is emended in later editions, thus :

> First sweare by thy best love, here, in earnest

which alteration makes it a little smoother. Leaving aside for the present the wrenching of the stress in the last word, the

---

(1) *Works,* edited by Edmund Gosse (1884), vol. I, pp. 340-I.

1633 reading provides us (unless we choose to make « sweare » a dissyllable) with the only instance of initial truncation to be found in this piece ; Donne, then, proves very sparing in the use of this licence, abundantly authorized by Chaucer's example, and he never recurs to the certainly Lydgatian, if doubtfully Chaucerian, licence of truncation at the caesura.

Supposing « earnest » to be normally accented, the line would be, not one, but two syllables short; however, that word rhymes with « best », and Donne probably wanted his reader to shift the stress to the last syllable. Similarly in line 20 :

> Deigne with a nod, thy courtesie to answer.

« courtesie » (in the meaning of « curtsy ») is probably dissyllabic, and « answer » is accented on the second syllable to rhyme with « courtier » (reckoned as three syllables). I think it far more likely that Donne offered violence here to the language than to the metrical design, and consider line 20 at any rate as a regular, though not smooth or pleasant, deca-syllable.

What gives additional support to this opinion is the absence of any couplet with feminine rhymes. Of an hypermetrical syllable at the caesura there is only one instance (l. 28) :

> Of refin'd manners, yet ceremoniall man,

and very few instances of trisyllabic feet :

> In prison, and here be coffin'd, when I dye ; (l. 4)
> The sinewes of a cities mistique bodie ; (l. 8)
> Here gathering Chroniclers, and by them stand (l. 9)
> Of thy plumpe muddy whore, or prostitute boy (l. 40)
> Charitably warn'd of thy sinnes, dost repent (l. 50)
> The Infanta of London, Heire to an India ; (l. 58)
> He them to him with amorous smiles allures, (l. 73)
> Then the wise politique horse would heretofore, (l. 80)
> Now leaps he upright, Joggs me, & cryes, Do you see (l. 83)

The gentlest slurring will turn « prison » into a monosyllable, « gathering » and « amorous » into dissyllables, if they are not such already ; « prostitute » will resist this process somewhat more on account of the meeting of the *t*'s ; but after all the *i* is a short unstressed vowel between two consonants in a polysyllabic word and may be sacrificed to metrical regularity, as may, with less difficulty, those of « charitably » and « politique » ; the elisions of « the » before « Infanta », of « Infanta » before « of », and « to » before « an » (« India » is trisyllabic and rhymes with « away ») may severally claim justification by innumerable precedents, and only their reunion in one line deserves notice ; the elision of « he » before « upright » is also traditional, and that of « do » before « you » is a fact in spoken English. The only trisyllabic foot in this list which defies slurring is the last one of line 8, for « bodie » is stressed on the second syllable to rhyme with « tie », as elsewhere « earnest » rhymes with « best », and « answer » with « Courtier ». It would not, however, be unlike Donne the equivocator to make « bodie » a sort of metrical bat, now bird and now mouse as it suits his purpose : plain « bódie » if you enquire how many syllables there are in the line, but « bodíe » if you ask how it may rhyme with « tie ».

Gray did not err when he said that « the number of syllables is equal throughout » in Donne's satires. The exceptions recorded above did not shock or puzzle the classical poet and metrist ; *a fortiori* we should not boggle at them. There remains to make good the word « only » prefixed by Gray to « the number of syllables » in his statement, and see what he meant by : « no regularity in the pause, nor in the feet ». Here are four lines, consisting each of ten syllables, neither more nor less‘ and

which refuse to fall, not only into five iambs, but even into five
feet, be they iambs, trochees, pyrrhics, or spondees :

> Wilt thou grin or fawne on him, or prepare (l. 23).
> For better or worse take mee, or leave mee : (l. 25).
> Sooner may one guesse, who shall beare away (l. 57).
> Perfect French, and Italian ; I replyed, (l. 103).

To these four we may add a fifth line, in which slurring, as
we have noted, disposes of an extra syllable :

> Charitably warn'd of thy sinnes, dost repent (l. 50).

Of course nothing in these lines will prevent Mr. Melton (2)
from scanning them as pure five-foot iambs ; his "flat iron" (3)

---

(2) *The rhetoric of John Donne's verse*, by Wightman Fletcher
Melton, Baltimore, J. H. Furst Company, 1906. This dissertation for
the Johns Hopkins Ph. D. is a sort of *reductio ad absurdum* (quite
unintentional) of Professor Bright's theory of " secondary word-
accent in English verse ", a theory which, more soberly handled,
expresses one aspect of the complex prosodical truth. Mr. Melton
indeed allows that the trochee may be substituted for the iamb in
the initial foot, and even after the caesura ; but he forgets this
admission every time it suits his purpose, so that three fourths of
his examples prove nothing. For instance the following lines of
Milton are called upon to show that in dissyllabic words the suffix
may bear the stress :

> As when two polar winds *blowing* adverse (P. L., X, 289)
> With lucky words *favor* my destin'd urn, *(Lycidas,* 20)
> Unsung ; or to describe *races* and games, (P. L., XI, 33)
> Tended the sick *busiest* from couch to couch *(P. L.,* XI, 490)
> Silence, and sleep *listening* to thee will watch (P. L., VII, 106)

Only three of the lines quoted by Mr. Melton from Milton in this
connexion need not be summarily dismissed :

> Among *daughters* of men the fairest found *(P.R.,* II, 154)
> By the *waters* of life where'er they sat *(P.L.,* XI, 79)
> But to *vanquish* by wisdom hellish wiles *(P.R.,* I, 175)

The true-born Englishman will decide whether he prefers to shift
the stress or not in "daughters", "waters", and "vanquish". I shall
merely point out that these lines, all three very melodious if read
"like prose", *may* be considered as stray survivals of Chaucer's,
Spenser's, and Donne's non-iambic decasyllable, about which see
infra.

(3) The phrase is Professor G. C. Moore-Smith's in his caustic
review of Mr. Melton's book *(Modern language review*, 1907-8, vol. III,
pp. 80-82).

will smoothe away any creases. In l.23 such unimportant words as "grin" and "fawne" shall go unstressed, while "or" shall be honoured twice (4). In l. 25 "worse" shall dispose of its stress in favour of the preceding "or". In l. 50 "sinnes" and in l. 57 "guess" shall do the same in favour of "thy" and "who", though the sense does not require that either the possessive adjective or the relative pronoun should receive emphasis. In l. 103 "French" shall carry no stress, but "and" shall carry one.

Professor Saintsbury would not deal with such metrical cruxes in Mr. Melton's high-handed manner ; if it were not impertinent for me to praise him, I should say he has far too much ear and feeling. Yet I doubt whether he explains them adequately when he says : "Donne, recognizing the classic practice of equivalence and substitution, used it in experiment more freely than wisely, as upon the *corpus*, admittedly *vile*, of satire" (5). Substitution, under one name or another, especially that of the trochee for the iamb, undoubtedly exists in English

---

(4) Not without some pang in Mr. Melton's heart, however, since his own pet theory on Donne (as distinct from Professor Bright's general theory which he adopts with such indiscreet enthusiasm) is that of "arsis-thesis variation", which he states thus on the poet's behalf : "When a word, a syllable, or a sound, appears in arsis, get it into thesis as quickly as possible, and *vice versa*". Though "or" disobeys this rule in ll. 23 and 25, "mee" obeys it in the latter, provided of course we scan it like Mr. Melton.

This theory of "arsis-thesis variation" contains one ounce of truth to a pound of violence to language; but since its exaggeration will be discounted at once, we may thank Mr. Melton for bringing it forth with great, yet jubilant, labour. He no doubt deserves the qualified praise bestowed upon him by Professor Saintsbury *(History of English prosody*, II, 161, n. 1) and Professor Grierson *(Metaphysical lyrics*... p. xxiv). Personally I could wish Mr. Melton's theory were fully established ; it would prop mine about our poet's craftsmanship. Indeed Mr. Melton goes so far as to say : " If Donne sinned it was rather in excess of care than in carelessness " (p. 87). I should follow him there, at least part of the way.

(5) *Op. cit.*, II, 161.

verse, in Elizabethan verse, in Donne's verse ; it might account
for peculiarities in many lines of his satires, of this satire. Yet
could even Donne be charged with trying to pass "guess, who"
or "French, and" upon us as trochees, in spite of the caesura
which says so clearly they are not feet at all, but the final
syllable of one foot, or section, and the initial syllable of the
next ? Feminine (lyric) caesura is welcome in an iambic line
when it falls within an iamb ; within the reverse foot it ruins
the metrical design irretrievably.

One might perhaps accept Professor Saintsbury's explanation
if the above-quoted lines were freaks of Donne's without any
precedent in English poetry. But, as Gray pointed out, Donne's
Satires stand in close relation to Spenser's *August* (6) where, not
a minority, but the large majority of the decasyllables, will not
fall into five feet. I quote a few instances :

> With pyping and dauncing did passe the rest (l. 10)
> Ah ! Willye, now, I have learnd a newe daunce (l. 11)
> Of Beres and Tygres, that maken fiers warre (l. 28)
> Thereby is a Lambe in the Wolves jawes (l. 31)

referring the reader to Professor Emile Legouis' exhaustive study
for the others, and for the full pedigree of these anomalies (7).
Briefly, they appear in Chaucer :

> Withouten hyre, if it lay in his might *(Prologue,* l. 538*)*

and reappear (in the welter of XVth century prosody they cannot
be distinguished from other and graver departures from the
metrical norm) in Wyatt :

---

(6) Professor Saintsbury has little to say about this *Æglogue,* and
that little concerns the stanza form, not the internal structure of the
lines (*op. cit.*, I, 356).

(7) *Quomodo Edmundus Spenserus ad Chaucerum se fingens in eclo-
gis "The Shepheardes Calender" versum heroicum renovarit ac refecerit.*
Paris, G. Masson, 1896 (pp. 45-60).

> Without eye, I se ; without tong I playne
> *(Tottel's Miscellany,* Arber's reprint, p. 39)

and Surrey :

> Till we came to the hill whereas there stood
> *(The second book of Virgil's Æneid,* l. 929.)

In 1575 Gascoigne, though he recognizes as a fact that the English poets of his time use no other foot than the iamb, regrets the greater freedom which had existed before :

« Note you that commonly now a dayes in English rimes (for I dare not cal them English verses) we use none other order but a foote of two sillables, whereof the first is depressed or made short, and the second is elevate or made long ; and that sound or scanning continueth throughout the verse. We have used in times past other kindes of Meeters, as for example this following :

> *No wight in this world, that wealth can attayne,*
> *Unlesse he beleve, that all is but vayne »* (8).

Each of these two lines is decasyllabic, but the iambic-ana-pestic rhythm would be unmistakable even if Gascoigne's system of typographical accents and accompanying diagram did not place it beyond cavil that for him the lines fell into four feet, not five. The only difference between him and Spenser or Donne in this respect is that he rather despondently advised his contemporaries « to take the forde » as they found it, while Spenser once and Donne several times tried to revert to former liberty.

If the reader agrees that I have made out my case about those five lines of *Satire I* (ll. 23, 25, 50, 57, 103), he will further grant that they are not merely a few scattered rocks in an iambic sea. Some twelve other lines, though they might be made to conform to the five-foot type by dint of stress-shifting

---

(8) *Certayne notes of instruction concerning the making of verse or ryme in English, written at the request of Master Edouardo Donati.* Edited by G. Gregory Smith in his *Elizabethan critical essays,* Oxford 1914 (vol I, p. 50).

or foot-substitution, read much better as four-foot decasyllabics. For instance, in ll. 41 and 77 :

> Hate vertue, though shee be naked, and bare ?
> And as fidlers stop lowest, at highest sound,

Mr. Melton no doubt would have us pronounce « nakéd » and
« fidlérs », (9) and he might invoke the rhyme-words mentioned
above : « bodíe », « earnést » and « answér ». But, unless we
also give him « French ánd », etc..., what purpose will this
concession serve ? What is the good of passing an Act of
Uniformity if you are to except individuals from its operation ?
And why not fifteen exceptions as well as four ? Besides, the
purely iambic lines, those where no substitution of foot or
wrenching of stress is at all required, number only fifty-two in
this satire ; their tyrannizing over the others would be all the
harder to brook for their being, not a majority, but a mere
plurality, unless the English electoral system also obtain in
English prosody. — Here are, without further comment, the
other lines which I should scan as falling into four sections
each :

> Shall I leave all this constant company, (l. 11)
> (If thou which lov'st all, canst love any best) (l. 14)
> Why should'st thou (that dost not onely approve (l. 37)
> Whither, why, when, or with whom thou wouldst go. (l. 64)
> Now we are in the street ; He first of all (l. 67)
> So to the most brave, stoops hee nigh'st the ground (l. 78)
> Saying, him whom I last left, all repute (l. 95)
> (Which understand none), he doth seeme to be (l. 10)
> Hee quarrell'd, fought, bled ; and turn'd out of dore (l. 110)

In the *Songs and Sonets* such decasyllables are few and far
between, but some of them would prove unquestionably non-

---

(9) That is, if he did not prefer to tamper with the text so as to
make it agree with his theory of arsis-thesis variation (*op. cit.*
pp. 181-2).

iambic, even without the corroborative evidence of the *Satires :*

> I would have that age by this paper taught

(The Relique, 1. 21 ; there in no excuse for making « that » emphatic) ;

> Must learne, by my being cut up, and torne :
> > *(Loves exchange,* 1. 39) ;
> From us, and our cares ; but, now 'tis not so.
> > *(A Lecture upon the Shadow,* 1. 11) ;
> Once I lov'd and dy'd ; and am now become
> > *(The Paradox,* 1. 17).

And as those supposed five-foot lines have only four feet, so several octosyllables will fall into three sections instead of four :

> That my selfe, (that is you, not I,)
> > *(The Legacie,* 1. 10) ;
> That she knowes my paines, least that so
> > *(Loves exchange,* 1. 20) ;
> When my grave is broke up againe
> > *(The Relique,* 1. 1) ;
> If this fall in a time, or land,
> > *(Ibid.,* 1. 12) ;
> Thou art not so black, as my heart,
> > *(A Jeat Ring sent,* 1. 1).

It seems hardly necessary to analyse the effect of the caesura on the distribution of syllables between feet, or sections, in all those lines, octosyllabic as well as decasyllabic. I shall only refer the curious reader once more to Professor Emile Legouis' study of Spenser's *August* ; the same remarks apply to Donne's non-iambic lines as to those of his great predecessor.

To conclude, Gray gave us the whole matter in a nutshell, and detailed examination vindicates his theory in every particular. That it will explain every abnormal line of Donne's, I do not of course assert ; but it will explain more than any other single theory I have read so far. And it frankly recognizes, instead of destroying, the peculiar beauty of such a line as:

When my grave is broke up againe.

APPENDIX B

Donne undoubtedly addressed to Mrs Herbert one of his verse letters, *Mad paper stay, and grudge not here to burne*, one of his elegies, *The Autumnall*, and a sonnet, *Her of your name, whose fair inheritance*, besides many prose letters, only a few of which were printed by Walton. Gosse, *Life of Donne*, II, 26, states that *The Primrose* was also written to Mrs Herbert. Grierson, *Works of Donne*, II, xxiv-xxv, adopts this view, and, since *The Blossome*, *The Dampe*, *The Funerall*, and *The Relique*, recur repeatedly together with *The Primrose* in the manuscripts, he conjectures that the five of them have a common origin. But his arguments seem to me more ingenious than convincing.

The 1635 and later editions of Donne add to the title of *The Primrose* this precision: *being at Montgomery Castle, upon the hill, on which it is situate ;* now Montgomery Castle was the home of the Herberts; therefore the lady alluded to in this poem was Mrs Herbert. — It is true, as Professor Grierson himself notes, that the full title is found neither in the 1633 edition, which he generally considers the most trustworthy, nor in any of the mss. — « But it is easier to explain the occasional suppression of a revealing title than to conceive a motive for inventing such a gloss ». — This remark carries some weight, but is answered elsewhere by the same editor (II, cxxxix) : « I do not attach much importance to this title [*Sr Walter Aston to the Countesse of Huntingtone*]. Imaginary headings were quite common in the case of poems circulating in manuscript. Poems are inscribed as having been written by the Earl of Essex or Sir Walter Raleigh the night before he died, or as found in the pocket of Chidiock Tichbourne. Editors have occasionally taken these too seriously. » May it not be that the 1635 editor, aware of Donne's friendship with Mrs Herbert, made a guess at random? If so, the later editors merely followed him, as they usually do.

The only other piece of evidence in favour of the « sequence »'s being addressed to Mrs Herbert is found in *The Relique*, l. 17 : when, the poet says, he and his love are canonized, she shall be « a Mary Magdalen ». Now Mrs Herbert's Christian name was Magdalen. Then the poem was written to her. — It would take a very humble Christian female to be pleased with such a compliment, unless she had notoriously fallen into the same errors as the saint. Now Mrs Herbert was an aristocrat, every inch of her, and the lady in her always qualified the Christian. When Donne, in the sonnet mentioned above, did venture to play, most respectfully, with the name of his noble friend, he was careful to state that to the « Devotion » of her patron saint she added « Innocence ».

Against the identification of the « mistress » addressed in the « sequence » with Mrs Herbert, the tone of three at least of the poems protests. Professor Grierson himself confessedly hesitates to connect *The Dampe* with this lady on account of the scorn it breathes. But while mere scorn might plead Petrarchian precedents, there is no excuse for the obscenity of the last four lines if the woman whom the poet invited to try on him her « passive valour » had a stainless character and added to her noble birth true nobleness of mind. In *The Blossome* Donne veils his cynicism somewhat more ; yet can we avoid reading a coarse innuendo in ll. 31-32 :

> Practise may make her know some other part,
> But take my word, shee doth not know a Heart ?

And the concluding stanza shows us a very youthful Donne, quite unconfined as yet in his amours, and not at all prepared to pine for any one woman who happens to be "stiff", while so many of her sex prove more pliant ; he gives his heart a *rendez-vous* in London, twenty days hence, and asks it to arrive fresh and fat, because :

> I would give you
> There, to another friend, whom wee shall finde
> As glad to have my body, as my minde.

Gosse, I, 75, makes a curious mistake about the meeting in London, but rightly styles her for whom the poem was written, 'the lady of the moment". To the poet at any rate she was that, and only that ; or, else, the dialogue between Donne and his heart no more refers to an actual incident than his other dramatic lyrics need do. Similarly, in *The Primrose* the scenery may well be imaginative. And even in this last piece the tone adopted by Donne hardly agrees with our idea of Mrs Herbert. The conclusion, wrapped up in a mystical theory of numbers, advances two propositions, the second of which improves upon the first :

> Each woman may take halfe us men ;
> . . . .
> . . . . women may take us all.

Professor Grierson comments thus : (1) united with man woman will be half of a perfect life.... (2) she may claim to be the whole in which men are included and absorbed. We have no will of our own. - I do not deny that the lines may be so construed, but think their meaning is both simpler and coarser : (1) each woman has a right to half the males of her species ; (2) "Or, if this will not serve *her* turne", each woman may take to herself as mates all men. This explanation is supported by the maxim in *Communitie*, on which I have commented in this essay: "All, all may use". If the reader frees himself from any preconception that the poem is addressed to Mrs Herbert, I dare pit my interpretation of these lines against Professor Grierson's, however rash it generally is to challenge him. And as regards his general explanation of the cynical element (which he minimizes but does not wholly exorcize) in *The Primrose* and its companion pieces, to wit that Donne has a difficulty "in adjusting himself to the Petrarchian convention" and that "his passionate heart and satiric wit" tend "to break through the prescribed tone of worship", it is no doubt true, so far as it goes ; but, while it accounts for the internal contradictions of these poems, can it reconcile the indecencies in them with the reputation of the lady for whom they are supposed to have been written ? True, Sidney himself once breaks off his moan, and gives utterance to this very unspiritual sentiment : since "Stellas selfe" is her soul,

> Let Vertue have that *Stellas* selfe, yet thus,
> That Vertue but that body graunt to us.

(Sonnet LII, ll. 13-14. — Us means the poet and love). But even here Sidney hardly anticipates Donne's audacities ; besides, the former was a duke's grandson and could address an earl's daughter somewhat freely without the fear of being cudgelled by servants ; there was no such equality between the daughter of Sir Richard Newport and John Donne.

To sum up, these five poems do not, to my mind, constitute a "sequence" ; nothing proves that they were written to the same woman ; nothing even proves that any of them was written to a real woman ; they should be studied as artistic handlings of lyrical themes, not as biographical documents in the narrower sense of these words.

89423

NOV 1 9 1970

NOV 1 9 1970